Law and Order Series

THE EMERALD CITY RUSTLERS

by

Peter Beck

ACKNOWLEDGMENTS

My writing journey has been profoundly enriched by the guidance and support of a remarkable teacher and mentor, Sutton Fox. Her talent as a writer and her unwavering support as my beloved daughter-in-law have been invaluable to me. She has been a constant source of inspiration, guiding and encouraging me every step of the way. Without her loving assistance and significant contributions, there would be no stories to tell or put on paper. I am forever grateful for her influence on my work.

My life partner, Sharon, has also helped me with sentence structures and punctuation and enhanced my stories further. She has also been my biggest fan and urges me to continue my journey into Western lore as a new writer.

The State of Texas in Crisis

This story is a new beginning for a long-overdue solution to Texas's rampant lawlessness, plaguing the very fabric of life in the cities and towns of that era.

It all began with an idea and a vision of a man steeped in the rules of law and justice. Chief Justice Bidwell is the ranking member of the Texas Supreme Court. He would begin fulfilling his vision by hiring two unique men destined to change how law enforcement officers fought and defeated the evilest of these marauders that plagued the landscape of Texas in 1875.

From the meager beginnings of an idea, we move on to the exciting possibilities if the right persons were joined together in harmony to administer and defend the laws of Texas.

The first of these unique lawmen would be a newly appointed Judge, Jericho Starr. He would be a man of many talents, and his lineage and heritage would produce a great leader. The other exceptional man would become a Chief Deputy, someone chosen from the ranks of the Texas Ranger, a man with the seasoned qualities of a long-time lawman named Jack Harden.

Both men would be chosen for their honesty, dedication to duty, toughness, and unique abilities with guns and fists, which had never been seen before in the great State of Texas.

Table of Contents

INTRODUCTION

In June 1875, the Texas Coastline suffered two monstrous hurricanes.

The first of these storms came ashore near the town of Galveston. It continued northward until reaching its final destination, where it slowly dissipated. However, the heavy rains that fell while on and during its path caused heavy flooding throughout vast areas of the state. This first hurricane would impact the lives and fortunes of many Texans miles from its beginning.

Right on the heels of the first storm, a second hurricane developed as it percolated in the Gulf of Mexico long before coming ashore to strike the Texas Coast near Beaumont. This storm would take a westward path along the South Texas Coast, and unfortunately, this area of the State was fraught with cactus and sagebrush that grew in abundance, a barren nothingness to slow the storm's progress.

Judge Jericho Starr is a newly appointed member of the Texas Bar Association. Today, he should be celebrating his appointment to the bench, but for now, he is traveling that barren stretch of nothingness and is right smack in the middle of this massive storm. He couldn't celebrate anything if he didn't get somewhere safe very soon.

CHAPTER ONE

"Damn, this blasted weather!" Jericho proclaimed, as he leaned forward on his horse to get some respite from the heavy winds and stinging rain.

His thoughts flashed back to this morning when he broke camp, and he was trying to rationalize the decision that brought him to this desolate part of the State and this vicious storm.

When he started this morning, only a soft rain fell, and there was nothing to worry about. A light rain wouldn't have alarmed him or caused him to change his plans.

But he couldn't have perceived the magnitude of his plight at that moment. After all, a little rain would always be welcome to help cut the dust off any road in Texas.

But Mother Nature was at her absolute worst this day, and he was up to his ass in some hellish weather. The storm raged and buffeted him without mercy, and he wished he and his horse were somewhere safe and far away from this miserable storm.

Jericho mused inwardly to himself. You sure are stubborn. You had to rush right into this damn storm trying to get somewhere fast. Now you're wishing for a miracle to save you! Stop wishing and start thinking of how to get out of this mess.

Pulling his Stetson down tight, he set himself and doggedly continued buckling the storm's force. Right now, he couldn't stop in the middle of nowhere.

Jericho had to divide his attention as he rode. There was the storm he had to contend with and the road of sorts that was fading fast into something less than a muddy hidden path.

He was getting uptight about his situation, and his shoulders ached. Rubbing his neck, he could feel the tension and tightness enveloping his muscles. He needed to relax soon, or his head would fall off.

Looking up into the face of the storm, he desperately searched the vista before him, looking for some relief. But nothing had changed; he was still in the midst of this God-awful road in the middle of nowhere, surrounded by nothingness.

Jericho's mind switched to something else as he thought of the meeting with his new boss about his latest assignment. He remembered what his boss had said when he gave him his first assignment. Thinking aloud, he mumbled under his breath, I could blame my boss for my predicament, but shaking his head, he owned up to his plight today. His situation was his own.

He was remembering what had transpired after his conversation with Judge Bidwell. The Judge had urged him to travel to the town of Lufkin to interview a friend of his, Captain Harmon.

As he continued to battle the storm, Jericho mulled over the events after the swearing-in ceremony. His first order of business was to get to the town of Lufkin. He had a new job as his deputy that needed to be filled. That had been his intent these past few days of hard riding, but the storm had placed a roadblock on his attempt to reach his goal.

Jericho shook his head to clear the rain from the brim of the Stetson, and his mind returned to the present and his sad situation.

He scolded himself. Why was he so upset? He could have stayed another few days in Houston or at the campsite this morning. But, of course, he had no idea what would take place. Jericho wondered when he had started blaming others for his judgments and said to himself, "Oh, *for Christ's sake, suck it up and get on with it."*

Stopping shortly, he took out his bandana, wiping the rain out of his eyes. Enough of this crap, he mumbled to himself. After all, thinking and doing were miles apart sometimes. Hunching his shoulders and ducking his head, he put his thoughts into action and gigged his horse forward.

The slicker he wore leaked moisture, and he could feel the dampness soaking his clothes, adding to his discomfort.

The storm's winds surrounded him, escalating into a fierce swirling vortex with stinging-driven rains that buffeted and pummeled them from all sides. Jericho clung tightly to his horse's neck, seeking a respite against the storm's onslaught.

Jericho knew they were near the destination. His instincts regarding directions and distances were trustworthy.

He patted the horse lovingly but had to trust that his big animal's strong muscles would survive this ordeal and not get cramps or pull any of its hamstrings.

Thankfully, minutes later, he and the horse entered the outskirts of the town of Lufkin.

Jericho was very anxious to meet Captain Harmon. The man had impressive credentials. He was commander of the Ranger

Station and in charge of a company of Rangers. He was a proven leader. And from what his boss told him about this friend, Harmon would be a good candidate for the position Jericho needed to fill.

As he rode into town, he saw some locals feverishly preparing for the storm's wrath. He was sure the city had a warning that this monstrous storm was approaching.

The residents were feverishly trying their best to protect the stores and businesses and were nailing boards to windows, anything handy that would help shield them from flying debris.

Jericho surmised that these people chose to ride out the storm. They knew the impending urgency of the disastrous consequences to their town if they didn't stay and prepare. But he could see they were running out of one of their greatest allies, precious time.

Jericho noticed the winds had died to intermittent gusts. All that remained was his bewilderment and a hard rain. He knew rain without the damaging winds would be welcome in a town like Lufkin. But these weren't the normal spring rains. They were massive downpours produced by the outer rain bands radiating from the core of an enormous hurricane, and a deluge engulfed him and the town.

He could see the driving rain washing away any semblance of a street. Mud and puddles ankle-deep were all that remained. It was dangerous stuff. Hidden under the puddles would be holes, submerged rocks, and debris. He carefully urged the big stallion forward along the waterlogged streets. He guided his horse to the edges of the roads where possible, hoping for some solid footing for his horse.

Jericho spoke softly into the horse's ear, "Easy, big boy, it won't be long now. Shelter and oats can't be much further on this shitty road."

Jericho momentarily stopped at the corner of a building to wipe the water from his face.

He thought he heard noises and searched for movement along the boardwalks. Finally, he located the source of the noise. He could vaguely see several men huddled under the overhang of one of the town's buildings.

Jericho urged his horse forward to where he heard the sounds.

As he progressed to the town center, he quickly understood why the men had chosen that building. This particular building was set back further from the line of stores and businesses. The building's long overhang supporting the porch's roof provided the best shelter to keep these foolish men dry while they watched the storm's progress.

Jericho kept clear of the deepest puddles as he headed his horse toward the building.

The closer he got to the noises, the more the noises changed to distinct voices. But he couldn't understand what they were saying, which puzzled him. He believed them to be arguing. They were shouting to be heard above the thunderous sounds of the rain on the tin roofs of the surrounding buildings.

As Jericho approached the building's overhang, he stopped to hear and see the men more clearly and began shaking his head in wonder.

Crap, he was listening to nothing more than their rhetoric

Of all things to argue about, they were arguing about this crazy weather. But he had to be fair. It was a safe subject that usually started almost all conversations in Texas.

One of the locals shouts, "I've been around these parts nigh on fifty years. This is by far the most rain we've ever had."

A different voice challenges him, saying, "Maybe so. But do you remember two years ago? I thought the town was going to blow away. I recall there was quite a bit of damage before that storm finally left."

The rain had begun to let up, and Jericho noticed. Their rhetoric suddenly changed, if only for a few minutes. They began discussing whether the worst was over. But as quickly as they spoke, the hard rains returned to force, causing a monstrous downpour of epic proportions.

This was very different from the rain Jericho had just sloshed through. This was a heavy downpour, blanketing the town with sheets of water, coming straight down as a dark, angry curtain.

Jericho heard another loud voice proclaim, "Holy shit, would you look at that now? I can't see anything across the street through that wall of water."

The rain's onslaught was enough for Jericho. He wasted no more time sitting and listening. He had already witnessed how rapid the changes in the storm could be.

Prodding his horse forward, he stopped when he was directly in front of the porch.

The men assembled on the porch finally looked up to see a

shadowy figure and horse by the hitch rail. The wall of water made it difficult to distinguish clearly who had arrived through this storm.

Several men moved closer to the edge of the porch to get a better view of the horse and its rider. They looked shocked. The rider was clad in a blue slicker and blue pants with yellow stripes from hip to ankle.

Jericho didn't bother to flip the reigns to the rail. His horse would not move unless he gave it the command to move. He quickly reached down and patted the horse's neck, wanting to let the horse know he cared deeply for its faithful allegiance. Jericho looked down at the street below. All around the horse's hooves was a mass of foaming froth. He felt the water from the roof above cascade over him and onto the horse's haunches.

He needed to do his business and get his horse and himself out of this position quickly.

Those on the porch still stared, mumbling and arguing about the weather. And why would everyone venture out in this awful storm?

Looking at the assembly of men, Jericho yelled out, "You men on the porch. Where can I find shelter for my horse? And

I'm looking for a Ranger named Harmon?"

The rains were still creating a terrible racket. But one brave man stepped forward into the rain's downpour to tell Jericho, "There's a Livery a couple of blocks down on your right. You're in luck, stranger. This building is the Ranger Station. And Captain Harmon is inside."

Quickly, Jericho touched his hat, a gesture to signal his thanks.

And the water-soaked man quickly ducked back under the shelter of the porch.

Jericho turned his horse and headed where the man had pointed and urged his horse back into the sucking red quagmire.

CHAPTER TWO

On the porch, the assembly of men began to voice their wonderment. Who was this stranger? What fool would be out in this storm? Where had the stranger come from? They all watched as the rider and horse disappeared into the downpour until it swallowed them entirely from sight. Their conversation changed from the storm's progress to comments about the rider in blue. One of the men complained, saying, "What kind fool would be out in this weather?" Another man added, "The guy's got to be crazy trying to buck a storm like this. He's about to kill that fine-looking animal."

Everyone joined in the conversation about the mysterious rider. "What in God's name would anyone want to risk his life and his horse to reach their town? And what did he want of Captain Harmon?"

One of the men on the porch, a big, raw-boned man wearing a Texas Campaign jacket, ventured, "I recognized that blue uniform under the slicker that rider's wearing. It's a regulation Army issue. I saw plenty of the same kinds of duds at the Post in Houston. That's when the US Army supported Sam Houston's Exploration Army for a time."

Away from the chatter on the porch, Jericho found the Livery. He was thankful for the directions from the man back on the porch. Jericho urged his horse forward into the covered barn-like structure, which was a welcome respite from the rain he had promised.

Jericho dismounted and shed his rain slicker.

Taking a towel from his saddlebag, he began wiping the legs of his big animal. The horse's haunches were dry once he was satisfied with his effort. Hanging the towel over the stall nearest him, he retrieved a bottle of rubbing liniment from the saddlebags.

The Hostetter appeared and watched as the big man took great pains to care for his horse. The Hostetter knew it was all necessary maintenance, but he could also see that this man knew how to care for a horse.

Jericho looked up and saw the Hostetter watching him closely. A few more brush strokes to his horse's flank, he was finished and put his gear away in his saddlebags.

Jericho approached the Hostetter and began discussing with the Livery's owner what he wanted done for his horse.

When he was satisfied that the Hostetter knew his wishes and that his horse would receive the excellent care it deserved, Jericho flung the saddlebags over his left shoulder and was about to leave the stables.

Jericho called back, "The horse is named Brutus. He's been through hell today, so make sure he's kept warm and well taken care of. I'll be back later to check on him when my business is finished." Jericho was sure he had given the proprietor more than enough money to ensure his wishes would be fulfilled and continued on his way to end his business with Harmon.

Meanwhile, back on the porch, the conversation had changed. But it was more of the same rhetoric as before, the storm.

Jericho walked across the muddy street, dodging puddles, to reach the side where the building with the porch was situated. He made it a point to walk under the cover of the roofs of the town's businesses as much as possible. He was sick and tired of getting wet.

Thankfully, the rain had subsided at that moment, and only a drizzle was falling as he approached the porch with the citizens.

The men on the porch were startled and somewhat taken aback that the stranger in the blue uniform had reappeared behind them. "Is Captain Harmon still in his office?" Jericho asked.

Some men began to snicker, and one said, "He's in there, all right! And he ain't about to be going anywhere anytime soon."

Jericho nodded his thanks and started for the door into the Ranger Station. But before he was about to move past the men, one man demanded loudly, "What's your business with Captain Harmon?" The man's demands were rude and uncalled for, which riled Jericho.

But the man continued to provoke Jericho, saying, "What kind of fool are you? What the hell's wrong with you anyway? This storm isn't fit for man or beast! And if you had any common sense, you wouldn't even be in our town in weather like this."

Jericho gritted his teeth. He tried his best to ignore the rudeness and started to move past the man.

But he was met with more demands from the obnoxious

man, "Who the hell are you anyway? What's the Army got to do with the Harmon? Is the Army after anyone in our town?"

Jericho stopped abruptly and stared at the man who had challenged him. He glared at the man with a fixed, angry stare. Jericho was so irked that he had to speak through a clenched jaw, saying, "Look, asshole! I'm neither a fool nor stupid. I wouldn't be out on a horse in this miserable weather unless I had a damn good reason to travel."

But it's none of your business why I'm here. Or what I'm doing and who I want to see, now get out of my way!"

Then, the rude loudmouth did something foolish, which surprised Jericho. He stepped close to Jericho, directly into his face. The position the rude man took meant to impede and block Jericho's entry into the Ranger Station.

Jericho's eyebrows furled into a deep scowl, and his eyes flashed with anger. His glare focused on the stupid man standing in his way. He was tired from riding in the storm and fed up with the man's rude manners. Jericho again started for the door, dismissing the man's rudeness and ignorance.

But the loudmouth wouldn't be deterred. He moved to a position, put his hand on Jericho's chest, and then pushed hard to emphasize that he meant business.

That tore it all to hell. Jericho's last remaining bit of patience was gone entirely. Now he was pissed way beyond his threshold for anger. Jericho couldn't stand this loudmouth's stupidity any longer, stating, "Asshole, I told you to get out of my way!"

Without waiting for a response, Jericho moved quickly to his left and nimbly slapped the hand away as he side-stepped the outstretched arm of the rude townsman. For good measure, Jericho extended his big right hand and brought it back with a handful of the man's shirt front. Jericho gruffly yanked the loudmouth off his feet, dragging the rude man close to his face.

Jericho quickly observed the fear that overtook the dangling man in his fist. And the loudmouth's fear was soon warranted when Jericho pushed the loudmouth away from him with a mighty heave.

The startled man reeled backward. His arms flailed around as he tried to regain his balance, and that's when everyone on the porch observed a moment of Texas truth.

Narrow leather-soled boots, slick rain-soaked wooden planks, and a body off balance were a terrible combination to overcome. As a result, the man's body came to an abrupt stop as he fell heavily onto his back and_with nothing to stop his momentum. He bounced and rolled off the porch into the muddy street below.

The men on the porch were startled at first, but then they laughed at the man lying in the muddy street. They stopped abruptly when Jericho glared at the group of men and angrily challenged, "Is there anyone else who wants to stop me from going through that door?"

No one on the porch said a word.

They quickly stepped back, flattening themselves against the building's exterior, anywhere they could get as far away from the big stranger as possible.

With no further hindrance from the group, Jericho entered the Ranger Office. But as Jericho entered, it was apparent why the men outside had snickered when they said that Ranger Harden wouldn't be going anyplace.

Seated across the room behind a well-worn desk sat a man whose right arm was bound and wrapped in a sling. The man had a large gauze bandage encircling his head, covering part of his eye, and to boot, the man's right leg was splinted and wrapped to the crotch with another long gauze bandage.

"Well, come on in and stop staring. State your business!" the man behind the desk angrily growled. Then the man turned back to poking his bandaged leg that was propped up on the edge of the desk. He was using the end of a rifle cleaning rod to try to poke at something that must be bothering him under the wrappings. "God, that itches!" the old man complained.

Jericho just smiled and removed his rain slicker. He shook the moisture from the slicker and hung it on a peg on the wall to dry. Then he turned around and asked, "Are you Captain Harmon?"

"Yes, I'm Captain Harmon!" growled the scruffy, bearded man seated in a rickety old chair. " Who wants to know?"

Jericho eyed the bandages, trying to suppress a small smile at the seriousness of the poor man's plight. He asked, "What happened to you? It looks like you broke everything from your head to your toes wrapped in all that gauze."

Captain Harmon must have realized he hadn't been very hospitable about then. And he told Jericho, "Stranger, why don't you go over and get a cup of coffee? There's a clean cup on a shelf over the stove." But get right back over here, and then you can tell me who you are and what you want."

Jericho welcomed the offer of something hot. His damp clothes had chilled him, and after pouring himself a cup of coffee, Jericho returned to the desk and was about to sit when he remembered. He hadn't properly introduced himself.

Setting his coffee cup down on the desk, Jericho stood straight, cleared his throat, and stated in a crisp voice, "My name is Lieutenant Starr, Jericho Starr! And as of right now, I'm attached to the US Army's representative in Houston. I have been serving there as the Provost Marshall for the Texas Republic Exploratory Force. I'm here because your friend, Judge Bidwell, sent me."

The older man looked into Jericho's blue eyes, choosing what he was about to say.

"Sit down, Lieutenant Starr. I haven't told anyone what happened to put me in all these bandages, and you can be the first to hear the full story."

Jericho sat facing Captain Harmon. He felt the old lawman was about to burst from having to withhold his story for so long. And he was honored that the good captain was about to explain to him, a stranger, how his condition had come about.

Captain Harmon looked at his bandaged body and back to the Lieutenant, saying, "Sit back and make yourself comfortable. I needed you to sit so I didn't have to crank my neck to look up at you."

Jericho took Harmon's advice, sat back in his chair, grabbed his coffee cup, and waited for the captain's story.

CHAPTER THREE

Captain Harmon's brow furled in deep thought as he began to talk about his accident, saying, "My tale of woe began last week. It all started when a squad of my Rangers and I were headed out to follow up on a tip to where a band of renegade Indians were supposed to be hiding." We've been after this bunch for quite a while for raiding a wagon train bound for Houston. They killed several of the drivers during their raid, and they had been terrorizing small homesteader settlements for some time. They always seemed one step ahead of us in our searches for them, but now that I knew where they were holed up, I couldn't pass up a chance to bring those heathens to justice. We neared the camp where they were hiding. One of the renegades who must have been a lookout saw us coming and took a shot at me."

"That back-shooting son-of-a-bitch's bullet creased my head, and it knocked me off my horse. As I hit the ground, the fall broke my collar bone, and in all the excitement, my damn horse stepped on me and broke my leg to boot."

Jericho couldn't contain his smile any longer and began laughing. That's what I call one hell of a tale!" Then Jericho abruptly stopped and became serious again, asking, "Captain, what about that Indian who shot you?"

Looking up with a satisfied smirk, the captain replied, "He's dead!

My men thought I was dead and rode on ahead into the Indian's lair and captured or killed most of the renegades. While my men were in their camp, that stupid Indian who shot me must have thought I was dead and rode down from his sniping spot to check my body for loot. Big mistake on his part, I can tell you! I might have been wounded and broken, but I'm a tough old bird. I shot him when he was fifty yards out with my Sharps Rifle. My shot blew that back-shooter clean off his horse, and he was dead long before his body hit the ground."

Captain Harmon seemed satisfied with his rendition of his tragedy and repeated the question. "Now, what's on your mind? And please tell me what's so important that you had to risk life and limb to be out in this miserable weather. Since you're all dressed in those Army duds, I must ask, what does the Army want from the Rangers now?"

Jericho took a sip of coffee and said, "I was sent here looking to hire myself a Special Deputy, and my new deputy will also become a U.S. Marshall for the State of Texas."

Jericho relaxed and continued his report, "The judge has appointed me to become a Circuit Judge, a sort of a troubleshooter for the State of Texas."

"And as soon as I find a good man to be my deputy, I can start my duties."

Captain Harmon put down the cleaning rod and raised his eyebrows, asking, "Lieutenant, what are you and your deputy supposed to do that the rangers haven't been doing?"

Jericho momentarily thought as he replied, "Being a judge and having a good deputy to help me, we will work close together, issuing judgments on the spot. That would mean the Rangers and other Lawmen won't have to wait weeks or months for a judge to appear and settle their cases."

Jericho gave Captain Harmon a chance to absorb what he had just said. And then he told him. "Judge Bidwell is well aware that the ranger's assignment at this time and your job have been chasing down and hopefully ending these Indian uprisings. While the Rangers are trying to resolve these issues with the Indians, there is a real need for someone to take on the load of day-to-day law enforcement around the State. Another big problem has been that most of our cities' sheriffs only serve those who pay for their favors."

Jericho looked at Captain Harmon to see if he understood what he had offered and continued telling him, "That's why the other men like Judge Bidwell were called upon to create these positions, and I've been selected to be one of his judges. Many others at our Capital think that having a Judge and a deputy or a Marshall working together is the most effective way to provide more justice to all the towns in the territories of the State."

Captain Harmon sat for a moment without speaking, absorbing the information the man before him had told him. He could see the possibilities in what his friend, the judge, had proposed. This might work, he thought, and he looked up again to take a long, hard look at Jericho Starr.

Lieutenant Jericho Starr was an imposing and formidable specimen of a man. The captain guessed him to be about six feet two or three inches tall, with big, powerful shoulders, putting him at about two hundred forty pounds of hard-packed muscle.

Jericho had the kind of good looks that would make most women's knees buckle with just a smile and a nod from him in their direction.

Captain Harmon was quick to note in his assessment of Jericho Starr that, on the other hand, this man would elicit quite a different response in most men. His presence and the way he carried himself would make those same men give this man sway and a wide path.

The captain also noticed the gun Lieutenant Starr carried on his hip. It was a new Colt 45 Peacemaker.

He recalled that Colt Firearms had introduced this gun model just this past year. This Colt model was also a very scarce weapon at this time. Most law enforcement officers didn't have them, and he couldn't recall anyone in his town with such a gun. One other thing gave him pause. The lieutenant's Colt Peacemaker was encased in a low-slung, well-used gunfighter rig, tied securely to his right leg.

The captain's face reflected his thoughts as he furrowed his brow again. He knew most Army Troops were issued the standard single-action Navy Colts. But this model, the Colt Peacemaker, was a gun that could be used for rapid fire, with six bullets that rotated when fired. This gun was shorter and lighter than the Navy Colt's and could be drawn quickly.

Those facts made Captain Harmon's study of the man take a different line of thought. Standing before him was someone he would consider to be very deadly. Lieutenant Starr had the unique look of a man who knew how and when to use the Peacemaker. And it didn't take a genius to see that standing before him could be one of the most dangerous men he had ever known.

And now Captain Harmon had another problem. He had a town on edge, and some people might see Jericho as a threat and want to test this most impressive man. With his Colt Peacemaker, this man would challenge those who saw him as a conquest.

Jericho entered Harmon's thoughts when he reached into his tunic, retrieved a rolled-up oilskin, and removed what appeared to be a note or a letter from the casing.

Captain Harmon, "This letter is addressed to you! But it was written well before Judge Bidwell knew of your present condition. Jericho walked to the desk and placed the letter in front of the captain.

Captain Harmon looked at the letter and searched for something in his desk drawers. After a brief moment of fumbling around, he produced and donned a pair of reading glasses and read,

To: My Good Friend Captain James Harmon,

I hope this letter finds you well. It has been a long time since you and I were together with Sam Houston's Army. I want to tell you about a critical mission I oversee so I will get to the point of my message. The State of Texas has given me the task of forming a force of well-trained, professional lawmen and trustworthy individuals who will provide much-needed justice to the remote areas of our fledgling Republic. I thought of you immediately and perceived that you were the right man for this assignment.

Lieutenant Starr, the man bearing my letter, will be one of my new traveling Circuit Judges. I told him about you and how you would make an excellent Chief Deputy and a US Marshall. Please make haste to close your affairs and join me. Please allow Lieutenant Starr to accompany you to Fort Justice. I anxiously await your presence at the Capitol.

George Bidwell

Captain Harmon removed his glasses and put the letter down as he sat back in his chair, looking discouraged. "Jericho, I'm sure you can see that I'm in no shape to join anything or anyone in my condition, but I would have jumped at the chance if I could!"

There was a long pause, and no one talked. Captain Harmon seemed deep in his thoughts for those long moments. Suddenly, his face became animated as he smiled, saying, "I think I might have a perfect man for you."

"I have a ranger who works for me, and he's one hell of a man. He would be a great asset to you and your new assignment. My ranger's name is Jack Harden, but we call him Cactus Jack around here." He is the best of all the men I command, and I highly recommend Jack as my replacement."

Captain Harmon continued describing his Ranger. "Jack is my best tracker. He can track a gnat in a windstorm, he's someone you can always count on if you have to fight, and he's also the best man with a rifle and a pistol I have ever known. Jack has had this stupid love affair with his special-made Henry Rifle, and now he prefers the rifle to the sidearm he carries, a remodeled Navy Colt. You might have seen this model, and it's the Colt with removable cylinders."

"But Jack is not shy when he talks about himself. I'm sure he will bend your ear about that rifle. And he will brag plenty about his other abilities if and when you get to know him."

Captain paused momentarily with a frown, adding, " And you should know this about Mr. Harden: The man can be a handful at times, and he's been known to be a little self-indulgent. But I would be quick to add that when Jack commits to something or someone, he's the best man you could ever want to watch your back."

Captain Harmon stopped discussing Jack and asked Jericho, "If you're interested in meeting Jack, I'll send for him so you can see about this man for yourself."

Jericho didn't hesitate, "I'd be happy to meet Jack, this man you call Cactus Jack, and if he's half the man you say he is? I'm sure he'll be the right man to join me." The captain lowered his bandaged leg to the floor, swiveled his chair to face the outer door, and yelled out to the men still standing on the porch.

"Hey, out there on the porch? Go fetch Carlos and tell him I want to see him, pronto!"

Jericho heard a muffled response as he listened to the noise of someone running.

Five minutes later, a thin, brown-skinned man rushed into the office and stopped before the desk, breathlessly asking, "Senor Harmon, what do you want of me? "Carlos, fetch your horse and ride to the Stillwell ranch. I believe that's where Cactus Jack should be. Tell Jack to drop everything when you find him, tell him I want his ass back here on the double."

Without another word, the thin man turned quickly and hurried out the door to do the captain's bidding.

CHAPTER FOUR

Captain Harmon explained as he swiveled his chair around and refocused his attention on Jericho. "Jack's out at the Stillwell ranch looking into a report of Stillwell's cattle being stolen. We've had a rash of cattle being stolen over these past few months. I believe something more is happening here, and I hoped that Jack could get me a lead that my Rangers could investigate further."

Changing the subject, Captain Harmon continued, "It might take Carlos several hours to find Jack and get him headed this way, so while you're waiting, you can rest here in one of my cells if you've got a mind to. These bunks I have are a step up from sleeping on hard ground or in the mud. And with all this rain we've been having, you'll be a lot dryer and warmer for the night."

Jericho momentarily forgot his manners but recovered by saying, "Much appreciated, and Captain, where's a good place for a hot meal?"

"I like the food at MacArthur's Saloon." offered the captain. It's just down the street a bit. A big sign above the door says Mac's Place. Just go out the door, and you turn to your left. His place is about five buildings down on this side of the street. You can't miss it! His place will be the only place in town where there's any noise coming from its doors in this shitty weather. And I'm sure you won't have any trouble finding his place. You'll hear the place long before you see it." Jericho smiled at the prospect of getting some good food.

He told the captain, "Today will mark the end of my enlistment in the Army now that I have this new assignment. That calls for a little celebration on my part. I plan to have a good meal and a few drinks to toast the men I've served with in the Army these many years."

"You're right; that does call for a celebration," remarked the captain. "But I suggest that you carefully watch the going's on around you. Mac's place can be a bit rowdy sometimes, so be careful what you say or do and watch your back."

Then the Captain looked up, smiling at his guest, and said, "Jericho, if you were to cause me trouble, it would make me sad as hell if I had to keep you any longer than necessary." Captain Harmon started laughing at his words. "Remember this, Mr.

Jericho Starr. I have open cells for just those situations."

The good Captain got up, grabbed his crutches, and started for the door. He looked over his shoulder, commenting, " The place is all yours! I'm leaving now to go home to my wife and kids."

"My wife promised me stew. Venison stew. And her cooking is out of this world, and I'm a fortunate man to have her."

Jericho heard the fading sounds of the captain's crutches mixed with the rain that had begun again and the sound of the front door closing.

Jericho took a fresh shirt and pants from the saddlebags and began hanging the damp clothes he had been wearing on a peg near the Potbelly stove. He added firewood to the stove to ensure enough heat to dry his wet things come morning. He felt a lot better when he had fresh, dry clothes on, but he also felt the tiredness pull at him as he settled onto one of the bunks in an open cell. He began mulling over everything Captain Harmon had told him about Jack Harden. That's quite a name, he thought. I bet there's a hell of a story behind that name.

He tried to visualize Cactus Jack Harden as he closed his eyes to rest a bit. That was the last thing he remembered before the tiredness drained him and sleep overtook his senses. A little nap for Jericho would typically have been half an hour. But somehow, his little nap turned into four hours of dead-to-the-world sleep.

Setting up and stretching, Jericho thought *he must have been more tired than he had first perceived.* Then, looking back at the cell's bunk, he frowned, thinking that was about the worst bed he'd slept in a very long time.

Groggily, Jericho rose and again stretched to loosen the kinks from his body. He began rubbing the sleep from his eyes and yawned. He felt the rumble in his stomach and realized it was telling him how neglectful he had been about feeding the growling beast.

Grabbing his hat, Jericho headed in the direction of Mac's Place.

He was happy the wind had subsided quite a bit, but there was still a misty rain as he followed the directions to the Mac's Saloon. The saloon was just what Captain Harmon said it would be, loud and boisterous.

Laying his hands on the tavern's batwing doors, he stopped before entering.

He could smell the various odors attacking his nose, and he smelled the substantial order of tobacco smoke and stale beer, but there was also a faint hint of the rich aroma of good food being prepared within.

Jericho pushed on through the batwings doors and stopped just inside for a moment to assess the layout of the smoky saloon. Seeing what he was looking for, he headed across the room to the big, shiny walnut bar across the whole back of the building.

"What'll it be, soldier?" asked the bartender.

"What brings you to the fair city of Lufkin?" Another question from the heavy-set barkeep just before Jericho stepped to the bar.

Jericho thought a minute; he began to smile at something he remembered. That little speech he'd heard from Harmon before they had parted.

Jericho refocused on his present situation and said to the barkeep, "There are several good reasons for being in your bar tonight. For starters, I would like some good whiskey, and then later, I'll order something from your kitchen. Barkeep, I don't want to offend you but don't give me the stuff you serve daily. I want the special whiskey you have stashed under the bar for special occasions!"

For some reason unknown to him, Jericho assumed the barkeep was MacArthur himself and added, "Captain Harmon sent me here with his recommendations, and he bragged heavily about the great food and good whiskey that you serve here, MacArthur."

"Well, if the good Captain sent you, I have some special whiskey. I'm sure you will like this brand. He reached under the bar and brought out a bottle similar to the one he had sampled in Judge Bidwell's office. The barkeep poured a large glass for Jericho, saying, "I do keep this for special guests and occasions, and knowing Harmon, you've just become my exceptional guest."

"My real name is Henry McAllister! But everyone around here calls me Mac. And please call me Mac! The good Captain and I go back a long way. He's one of my best friends; he's been a good friend ever since I first came to Lufkin." The captain is quite a man, but he's busted up right now. Best Ranger I've ever known."

Jericho sipped the whiskey and deemed it excellent, and it sure was smooth going down.

Mac asked, "Now, what would you like to eat, soldier?"

Jericho could smell the aroma of the steaks being cooked somewhere in the back and proclaimed, patting his belly, "I'll have one of your thickest steaks! I could smell them cooking in your kitchen before entering your place. I like my meat cooked medium rare, and I'd like plenty of fried potatoes, greens, and some bread to go with it. And if you have any cherry pie, that will finish the meal nicely."

"Stranger, we have everything you just ordered. It'll be a few minutes before it's ready. The drinks are on me because you're a friend of the captain," Mac replied with a grin. Then, pointing to a table across the room, Mack said, "Set yourself down at that table yonder, and take the bottle with you and drink all you want. It's a pleasure to know you!" Mac said, puzzled, "By the way, just who are you?"

Jericho reached across the bar and took Mac's hand, saying, "Jericho Starr is my name, formerly Lieutenant Starr of the US Army. Tonight, I'm celebrating the end of my enlistment in the Army. I'll have a few drinks to toast the good men I've known while in the service."

"Good for you," laughed Mac as he pumped Jericho's hand, "From the looks of you, you're more than just any old soldier. You've got the look of a seasoned veteran who's been around. I bet there's plenty of stories to be told; you, my friend, have a certain look about you. It's_that special look of someone who's had his share of action on and off the battlefield."

"You might be right about that, Mac; the Army and I have seen our fair share of skirmishes, and I have the scars to prove it." Jericho quipped.

Jericho thanked Mac for the conversation and the bottle. He left the bar rail and went to the table that Mac had pointed out. The table was set somewhat out of the main action in the rest of the bar, which suited him just fine. He pulled out a chair and sat down to wait for his food as Jericho began to unwind from the day's events that lay behind him.

And Jericho relaxed for the first time in a harrowing few days.

When his meal arrived, he was on his third glass of whiskey, which smelled delicious. The steak was thick and juicy, and the potatoes were fried crisp, just as he liked.

Jericho had just finished the main meal and was about to devour the thick slice of cherry pie when he heard this threatening voice behind him proclaim.

"Hey, Soldier Boy! You're in my favorite chair, and that's my favorite table! Now, get up and get out of this bar! I won't tell you again. And if you're smart, you won't return to Mac's place if you know what's good for you."

Jericho turned to the sound of the voice. Standing glaring down at him was the man he had pushed and knocked off the porch at Captain Harmon's office that morning. This time, the would-be tough had a gun tied down in a gunfighter rig, and he had two other men with him who were set to brace him.

Jericho quickly assessed the situation and determined that he was about to have three men's deaths on his hands.

Captain Harmon's words came flooding back to him. Jericho, don't make any trouble tonight. I'll lock up all concerned and sort out the story later!

"I said, get up, asshole!" yelled loudmouth again. "I told you to get up. It's time someone taught you a lesson."

CHAPTER FIVE

"Nobody pushes me around, and you'll pay dearly for what you did to me on the porch of Captain Harmon's office today."

Jericho slowly stood up, knowing this situation could get ugly fast. He considered drawing his gun and fighting the three, but any good options were minimal. He resigned himself. He would probably have to kill the three, something he wasn't looking forward to having to do that night.

Suddenly, a booming voice from the rear of the saloon called out, "Don't anybody move! Keep your hands away from your guns."

Jericho half-turned to see who was talking, and from the corner of his eye, one of the men on his left, who was with a loudmouth, flushed red with fear.

Again, but much louder this time, the same loud voice proclaimed another warning. This time, Jericho could tell the difference. The booming voice had become a very menacing threat.

The man behind the loud voice yelled, "I told you to hold on. I didn't mean you could move your hands anywhere, and that means everyone in this bar."

The din of other voices in the <u>bar</u> ended in utter silence. No one moved or batted an eye at that exact moment.

The voice proclaimed his disapproval to the three men, saying, "Owen, you and Larry, move your hands away from those hog-legs. I want to see both of your hands up above your shoulders without your guns. "Lester!" the booming voice proclaimed, "I do believe you're about to see if you're as good with that gun as your mouth lets on. I think you've stepped into a big pile of shit! That stranger you were about to brace has the looks of someone who won't hesitate to put your lamp out for good."

All eyes in the saloon looked at the man with the booming voice, including the three men frozen in place. There was no talking; there were just stares.

Jericho slowly turned, careful not to draw fire from the man doing all the talking. He truly wanted a look at the man behind the voice.

Jericho saw a huge man sitting at a table by the batwing doors through the bar's smoky haze. He couldn't help but notice that the big man had a large Henry rifle that was not pointed at him but directly at the three men. Funny, Jericho thought to himself. That chair was empty when he was talking to Mac. The stranger must have come in a bit later than he had; otherwise, he was sure he would have noticed someone of that size before.

Jericho now realized that the rifle wasn't meant for him. He was sure that the gun was intended for his three antagonists. Jericho turned back to see what the three men threatening him were doing. Two men had their hands high above their shoulders, which made Jericho happy, seeing that both men's hands were a long way from their guns. But he also observed the naked fear in both men's eyes.

Jericho looked back at his newest friend, nodded to him, and said, "Mister, I don't know who you are. I can't thank you enough for stepping in when you did, and I appreciate your keeping those other two off me for now."

Jericho turned back and stepped forward to within a foot of the man who had just threatened him. Concentrating his full attention on the man in front of him, he returned the favor saying in a menacing tone, "All right, asshole! It's just you and me now.

Again, you've managed to piss me off properly. You now have my full attention, and you didn't learn much from our first meeting today. So, let's back up and start this shindig by telling me who you are. I'd like to know more about the man I'm about to kill?"

"I ain't afraid of you, soldier boy," snarled the loudmouth in return. "My name is Les Kinkade. Maybe you've heard of me? Most people in these parts know of me and my reputation as a fast gun."

Les Kinkade turned his head toward the big man with the rifle and yelled, "Big man, I ain't afraid of you either. You and I will have a score to settle when I'm done with this soldier boy."

Jericho was furious, and his cheeks turned crimson as he fumed. Knowing the big man had his back, he declared in a voice that could be heard above the bar's patrons, "Turn around and face me, Kinkade! I'm about to end this business that you just started."

Kinkade snapped his head back around quickly. His vision took in Jericho's flashing, angry eyes and the sinister look of a very pissed-off man with a gun. He was facing a man who also exuded the confidence of a man with no fear. Les Kinkade was looking into the dark blue eyes of death itself.

Jericho's anger was boiling over as he proclaimed, "My name is Jericho Starr, Lieutenant Starr to you, Mister Kinkade! I've taken a big dislike of the words from your mouth and your shitty attitude. Jericho quickly added, "I don't like bullies and won't put up with your disrespectful comments about the Army. I take unkindly to someone who is rude to strangers. I hold such a person as being contemptible. I've had all the crap I'm going to take from you this day, and if you're looking to die tonight. I'm just the man to oblige you."

Jericho stopped momentarily, thinking about the mess the fight would produce, and said, "But maybe you and I should take this squabble outside. I don't want your blood all over Mac's saloon floor.

At that moment, Jericho began inwardly chiding himself. *Damn it to hell*, he thought. *I've allowed this loudmouth to goad me into a raging fury. Any bloodletting on my part would surely make Captain Harmon unhappy, especially if it meant he would kill any of the town's citizens.*

Even though he had someone backing him, the situation still looked bleak. No matter what might happen tonight, it was about to hamper his plans to leave the Ranger Station with the new man tomorrow.

Rolling options over in his mind, Jericho came upon an idea that might work. "Just hold on a minute, Kinkade!" Jericho demanded. "I have a better idea than just killing you outright. Let's you and me make this into a contest to see who has the fastest gun. You have been telling everyone how fast you were with that gun, but I'm sure I'm faster than you!"

"I want to set up a little test of skill that should prove just who's the best man with a gun. And when our little contest is over, you'll still be alive, but if you're still unsatisfied, we can take our beef outside, and I'll put you in the ground for good."

Les Kinkade looked puzzled, not knowing what to expect. The challenge took him aback, and little seeds of doubt started to creep into his mind. He began wondering what kind of no-win situation he had gotten into. With the removal of his two partners from the mix, he knew he would be forced to face the stranger he had angered alone.

Looking over at his two friends, he thought *he really knew how to pick losers for partners.* At that moment, his two friends, Owen and Larry, had their hands above their heads, shaking in their boots. They were scared out of their minds and would probably wet themselves sooner or later.

Les jumped back, startled, as Jericho started across the room. Jericho paid him no mind and headed for the balcony stairs directly before them.

Kinkade lowered his hand to the butt of his gun, ready for any sudden moves, not knowing what to expect.

Jericho continued to walk toward the stairs, turning his back to Kinkade as he moved. He stopped quickly to look for something along the wooden rail and found just the crack he had been looking for. He took a silver dollar from his inside pocket and bent down for a closer at the rail.

Jericho began pounding the metal coin into a crack in the wooden rail with the butt of his gun. Turning and facing back around, Jericho began pacing a few steps beyond the table where he'd been sitting. He continued until he had paced off ten measured steps, stopped, and turned around. Jericho grabbed two nearby chairs and spread them in a line on either side of him to mark where he'd stopped.

When Jericho was satisfied with the set-up, he looked around for someone to help with this contest he had in mind. He settled on one of the many pretty barmaids standing by the bar.

Jericho walked towards the bar and stopped where the girls were standing. Jericho fished into his pocket, took out a five-dollar gold piece, and handed the coin to the girl he had picked out for the contest. Looking into her eyes, he smiled and said, "Pretty lady, I want you to help me. Please come with me to where that man over there is standing."

Jericho told the girl the contest rules. He pointed to the spot where he had placed the chairs. "When Mr. Kinkade and I get into position, I want you to face where we both can see the coin but stay out of the line of fire." Then, I want you to stretch your arm straight out with the coin at your eye level. Whenever the two of us are ready and squared off, you can let the coin drop anytime you want and miss; when this is all over, no matter what happens, you can have the five dollars for your trouble."

Seeing Mac behind the bar with a worried look, Jericho yelled, "Don't worry, Mac. Anything we break, I'll be paying for it. I'll settle up with you when this is all over."

Everyone in the bar stopped talking, and their eyes were on the two men as they got ready to open fire at any moment.

CHAPTER SIX

Jericho stood beside Les between the two chairs, facing the stairs where the coin was embedded. He challenged the man beside him, saying, "All right, Kinkade. I'm ready, are you?"

"Listen up. When that pretty lady I was talking with, drops the coin she has in her hand, we both draw our weapons and fire at that coin that I pounded into the wooden rail. Whoever draws first and hits the coin is the fastest draw. Is that OK with you?" Jericho demanded.

Kinkade's answer was curt and nasty, "I don't like you or your games, asshole, but for now, I'll play along. Let's get this over with." And Les Kinkade positioned himself slightly ahead of Jericho as he stared at the rail with the coin.

With as much bravado as he could muster, Les Kinkade proclaimed to the crowd in the bar, "You all know that I'm going to win. And when this little game is over, you'll all see who the fastest gun around here is. I'll be buying the first round for everyone afterward, that is, after I kill this stranger."

Jericho was watching Les closely. Kinkade was the type of man who would cheat, if possible, but Jericho didn't see anything Kinkade could cheat on or gain an advantage on.

Jericho looked over at Les, and he seemed ready and assumed a gunfighter's stance.

The noise in the saloon came to a complete halt. All eyes were on the girl with the coin. She took a deep breath, closed her eyes, and let the coin drop from her fingers.

Les Kinkade froze when he chanced a quick glance at Jericho. To his amazement and horror, he saw Jericho's hand become a blur of motion. As Jericho drew his gun, he fired it, and his bullet hit the coin, sending it flying off against the wall behind the stairs. And then there was another blur of motion as he slipped his Colt back into its holster.

There had been a breathless hush over the bar occupants while this challenge was happening. Everyone in the bar heard the gun go off, and a second later, the five-dollar coin hit the floor with an audible clink. Time was suspended for a brief moment. Everyone holding their breath exhaled all at once into one loud gasp.

Then someone in the crowd hollered out, "holy shit, that's the fastest draw I've ever seen!"

Another man ran over, picked up the coin, held it high, and proclaimed, "There's a hole in the coin's center. The stranger's bullet hit the damn coin square on!"

Everyone in the bar began to talk in unison, and everyone agreed; it was the fastest draw anyone had ever seen.

Jericho turned his head to look over at Les Kinkade. His opponent was riveted to the floor like a statue. His hand was still gripping his pistol to draw, but the barrel of his gun had not yet cleared its holster. Jericho also noticed Les Kinkade's face was ash white, and his eyes showed raw fear. His Adam's apple seemed stuck as he tried unsuccessfully to swallow his spit.

Staring at Jericho in disbelief, Les Kinkade knew one thing for sure. He was looking at death itself standing next to him. Les finally found his voice and began stuttering, "Mister, I mean Mr. Starr, I mean Lieutenant Starr, I'm sorry that you and I sure got off on the wrong foot today, and I'm so sorry for what I said about the Army. And please forget about everything that happened tonight. I promise I won't ever bother you again if you let me and my friends leave."

Without waiting for an answer, Les Kinkade and his two companions turned and ran for the exit. Lester was first as he crashed headlong through the batwing's doors on a dead run. The loud laughter and hooting from the bar's crowd trailed behind them. Jericho looked for the big man who had helped him as he searched the bar. Evidently, the man who had stepped up to aid him was gone. Jericho watched the three men disappear and let out an audible sigh. He was sorry he hadn't had a chance to thank the big man for saving his bacon.

The girl who had dropped the coin came over and began thanking him for the five dollars, saying, "Mister, I would have to work a whole month to make that kind of money hustling drinks." Batting her eyes up at him, she asked, "Honey, are you sure I can keep the five dollars? Is there anything else I can give you in return for all this money?"

Jericho smiled and nodded, saying, "It's all yours, miss. You did an excellent job dropping that coin, and you deserve the money for your troubles."

The girl looked dreamily at Jericho and smiled, saying, "Anytime you want something extra handsome, I'm all yours, and it's free. Mister, you make my knees weak, and I tingle all over just looking into your beautiful blue eyes."

Even though her offer was tempting, Jericho didn't want any more problems that night. He begged off with the excuse that he had somewhere else that he had to be.

Before he left the bar, he smiled and waved to Mac now that everything was settling back to normal. He began flexing his shoulders to help himself relax.

He almost forgot the pie and headed for his table. Jericho grabbed the dessert from his plate, shoved it into his mouth, and licked his fingers clean.

Thinking to himself, he thought. *I'm indeed glad everything worked out. I won't have to spend any more time in Lufkin after all.*

The following day, Jericho struggled to get up from the cell's bunk and wished he had slept on the floor. Looking back at the bunk, he thought he'd slept on softer rocks than that blasted bunk. He was sure of one thing: he wouldn't sleep on that bunk again.

Bending backward to relieve the kinks in his back, he began stretching and turning his body from side to side. When he was finally satisfied with the exercises' effects, he pushed open the unlocked door of the cell, making a beeline for the potbelly stove.

Jericho felt the full force of radiant heat before he arrived at the stove. He could see the cherry-red glow from a few feet away and thought to himself. *I'm sure glad that he had added plenty of wood to the fire before turning it in last night. That stove had done a great job overnight of keeping the chill and dampness out of the jail cells and office.*

Jericho grabbed a potholder to help open the firebox's hot handles. He looked in and saw that several large glowing embers were still present. He reached_into the firewood box and added several new pieces of wood as he restocked the coals to rekindle a healthy fire. He stood by the glowing stove for a while, absorbing the heat and letting the warmth permeate him until, at last, he became so warm he had to move back from it. There was almost too much heat, and he had begun to sweat.

Jericho wrapped a potholder around the near-boiled pot of coffee, poured himself a cup, and carried the pot to the back door. He emptied the remaining brew on the ground, muttering, "Damn it to hell. It was still raining." Dipping the coffee pot into the fresh rainwater barrel outside, he returned it to the office and made new coffee. He set the pot back on the stove to heat the fresh pot of coffee for when Captain Harmon arrived.

Jericho heard the captain arriving, his crutches making a soft plunking sound on the planking as he came through the office door. He watched as the captain plopped into his chair, and Jericho mused that Harmon had about as much grace as a cow with crutches.

Jericho left the stove's warmth, bringing the pot of coffee to the desk. He poured the new coffee into the captain's cup and then grabbed his cup. Retrieving a chair, he sat down to wait for this man called Cactus Jack Harden.

After much small talk about the captain's past association with Judge Bidwell and their exploits years before, a couple of hours had passed.

There was a loud knock on the door.

As the door swung open, a huge bear of a man stuck his head and shoulders into the opening and asked, "Captain, you want to see me?"

"Jack, come in, come in," the captain urged.

The large man ducked his head and entered. His body just about filled the doorway as he walked into the office. The big man approached the desk, grabbed another chair, looked squarely at Jericho, smiled, and sat down.

Jericho was momentarily speechless. The stranger who helped him at Mac's Bar sat in the chair before him. Jericho vividly remembered what had happened last night, and his thoughts flashed back, thinking, *Thank God the big man was there to help him last night.*

Jericho finally found his voice, saying to the big man, "Mister, I can't begin to thank you for all your help last night. You left before I could buy you a drink for your stepping in when you did. You saved me from having to kill anybody."

"What the hell are you two talking about?" barked Captain Harmon. "Jericho, did you go and do something last night, something I'm going to regret today?" asked Captain Harmon.

"No, no, nothing happened," replied Jericho. There was a little misunderstanding with some locals that was settled without harming anybody."

For the second time since announcing his presence, the big man spoke. "That, my friend, is a very misleading statement, and I believe there was more than a little misunderstanding if you ask me. That was quite a demonstration you put on, the big man said. I don't believe I've ever seen anything quite like it. And anything Les Kinkade and his sidekicks get mixed up usually turns out wrong."

"I sensed that you didn't want you to have to kill any of them, and after all, they may be bullies. They're just a bunch of fools with few brains. I knew you wouldn't want to kill anyone just to defend a bunch of words. Besides, those two men that Les had with him were just out-of-work cowboys. These guys punch cows for a living, and they're not much use as gun hands." Les has always been the instigator, and those two follow his lead. You were about to throw down on those boys, right?"

"I had no other option with the three of them about to draw on me, and I didn't know how fast they might be with their guns," Jericho replied.

The big man elaborated on the events of the night before and told Captain Harmon, "Captain, he's the fastest man with a gun I've ever seen. And you know I've seen some of the best anywhere, including me."

CHAPTER SEVEN

"The big man smiled, saying, "You can bet ole MacArthur will tell you the same story later.

"Captain Les Kinkade and his two dummy partners were about to make things real ugly at his place, and if this man hadn't come up with that trick solution, they would still be cleaning up the bloodshed in buckets. And the best part is that what happened last night might have put enough fear in Kinkade that he won't be so quick to brace strangers from now on."

Jericho listened to Jack's assessments of last night's events. Then he began to look at the big man sitting across from him. His first impression told him that Jack would be a formidable opponent in any fight.

Jack had to be three inches taller than himself and weigh a good two hundred and ninety pounds, outweighing Jericho by fifty pounds. All in all, Jack would be a formidable presence that presented a quandary for any criminal. Should they challenge such a person or run like hell as fast as possible? His size alone made him a commanding presence, and if Captain Harmon were right, Jack would be a real asset when and if they got into a challenging situation or a fight. Jack's size and muscles, as well as his guns, would sure come in handy.

Captain Harmon broke into Jack's conversation as he cleared his throat and began introducing, "Jericho, this here's Jack Harden! And Jack, this is the man I had you come back from your assignment to meet. His name is Jericho Starr, but you need to call him by his proper title, "Judge Starr!"

Jack stood up and reached out his hand. Jericho arose to meet him and extended his hand in the traditional hand of friendship. However, when Jericho tried to release his hold, Jack grinned and gripped harder.

Jericho had encountered this old trick before; it was a sure way to test a man's mettle and strength. Well, Mr. Harden, Jericho thought to himself, *I might have a little surprise for you. I've never been known to give up, and I've never been beaten at this game.*

And despite Jack's crushing hold, Jericho inhaled, smiled, and squeezed hard right back. Jericho's fingers started to throb, and the pain laced through his hand as his bones were tightened in Jack's vise-like grip. He could feel them rubbing together like he'd stuck it in a vise.

The pain pulled the muscles of his forearm taught. But not to be outdone, Jericho rotated his wrist and pressed his thumb hard into the back of Jack's hand. Then he rotated his bodyweight forward and stepped into the man's space, pushing him slightly off balance.

This move was just enough to make Jack shift his grip a fraction. Jericho now had the advantage, and he squeezed with all his might, and the knuckles on Jack's hand rolled together like dice at a crap table. Jericho looked into the big man's eyes, and his smile broadened.

Red-faced, sweat beading on his brow, Jack grimaced and released some of the pressure on Jericho's hand, breaking the grip of the handshake.

With the pressure released from their hands, both men began to open and close their fists to get some blood back into their numb fingers. Jericho started to shake his hand back and forth to help the blood flow and massaged his fingertips, wincing at the sting of restored circulation.

"That's some handshake you got there, Jericho!" With a nervous laugh, Jack said, "It's been a long time since someone bested me at my own game."

Both men looked at each other briefly, then smiled, grabbed their chairs, and sat back down.

Captain Harmon continued as if nothing had happened, stating, "Jack, Lieutenant Starr has come here to Lufkin seeking a Chief Deputy, and he needs that somebody to become his deputy right now."

"Judge Starr assures me that person will also become a full-fledged US Marshall working in Texas. We have discussed the Marshall's position at length, and the Marshall would have jurisdiction in and beyond the Territories and states that border Texas."

Jack fixed his gaze on Jericho and asked, "First of all, why me? And second, what's all involved in being your chief deputy?"

Jericho thought momentarily, then explained the letter and his disappointment to Jack, saying, "When I walked into the captain's office yesterday, I knew after looking at his condition he couldn't help me. And I was going to leave and look for someone else. That's when your Captain Harmon suggested you as his replacement. But before I go any further, I want you to understand that this position is very dangerous, and we'll be on the road for long periods. There will be times that we might be up against much larger forces, and there would be only you and I defending ourselves. Some jobs, such as distributing warrants and ruling from me, will be easy, but some will be hard. You might be all alone when tasked with arresting and escorting criminals."

Jericho felt he should explain the situation further: "The honorable George Bidwell, my boss, was given the authority to hire six new Federal Judges and six Deputy Marshals.

Five of those assignments have already been filled. And whoever I select as my Chief Deputy would complete the final pairing."

Jericho glanced at Jack to gauge his reaction to the information and then explained why he had visited Lufkin. "Judge Bidwell suggested that I contact Captain Harmon and offer him the position which brings me to today's meeting."

Jack looked embarrassed, his face flushed, and a look of surprise appeared as he looked over toward Captain Harmon, saying, "Thank you, Captain. I'm honored you thought of me."

Jericho liked what he saw in Jack as he gauged his reactions. Jack was especially pleased with how this man took pride in himself and yet was also a bit humble.

Jack's comment proved to Jericho that the man before him was the best candidate. "Judge Starr, when do I start? When will we be leaving?" He pushed back his chair and stood up, stating, " Let's get this show on the road, times a-wasting. I'm ready to go right now!"

"Whoa there, Jack. I don't know whether to be happy or sad you're leaving," Captain Harmon said with a bit of sadness. Still, he stated, "Jack, I expect you to conduct yourself with honor and be a credit to the Rangers no matter what you encounter or wherever this young man takes you. Get your gear together and say goodbye. Jericho told me he wants to leave at first light tomorrow."

"Yes, Sir, I'll be ready, bright, and early!" Jack replied.

Captain Harmon looked at Jericho and said, " As for you, Lieutenant, you could bunk in the jail cell for one more night if you choose."

Jericho quickly replied, "Thanks, but no thanks, Captain. I'll find somewhere else to bunk tonight. I have had all the misery I can stand from that miserable bunk!" Jericho grimaced to emphasize the discomfort the bunk had given him. Jericho saw Jack was about to leave and told him, "There will be some logistic items to be taken care of when we reach Fort Justice. Judge Bidwell will swear you in, and the paperwork transferring you from the Rangers to a Federal Marshal will be completed there."

"Looks like we've got a deal, partner," Jack said, reaching out to shake hands again and acknowledge his acceptance of the offer.

Jericho didn't hesitate and grasped the big man's hand. He knew his hesitation would mean weakness in the other man's eyes, but he was also relieved when Jack firmly clasped his hand, let go, and stepped away. The battle for dominance was settled, at least for the time being, he surmised.

Jack was almost at the door when he suddenly stopped.

He was thinking hard about something else he needed an answer for and asked, "What's the reason for a Judge and a Marshal being put together as partners?"

Jericho thought a long time before responding, "As I told you before, this job is very hazardous. Last year, Judge Bidwell swore in several new judges operating by themselves, and then they were sent to the troubled areas around the State."

"Our state's government officials assumed that the local sheriffs would support and uphold the laws these new judges ruled on. Every one of those judges is dead now, shot down by the very men they were trying to imprison, and in one case, killed by a local sheriff. Sadly, none of those new Judges were gun savvy; they had no one to support or defend them, and those good men are all dead because of that oversight."

Jericho let that information sink in before he asked, "I'll see you outside this office at dawn, Mister Harden. I will see you tomorrow, won't I?"

"You bet your ass I'll be there! A team of horses couldn't keep me away. And since we'll be partners now, we might as well dispense with all the formalities. Jack grinned as he announced over his shoulder, "Most people call me Jack or Cactus Jack!"

"It's Good to know you, Jack, and you should call me Jericho! "

Once Jack had left the building, Jericho and Captain Harmon resumed their conversation, which revolved around the person named Jack.

Captain Harmon questioned Jericho, saying, "Jack said you're good with that gun you carry, and I have no reason not to believe him. Jack would know a good gun hand when he saw one, but to be clear, Jack's no slouch when using his handgun. I've seen Jack in action several times before, and when he had to use that hog leg he carries, he has ended many a fool's life." He's very fast for a big man and quick on the draw with that hog-leg, and the best part is he hits everything he aims at. But as of right now, as I told you, he prefers that particular Henry rifle. "If and when the occasion arises, Jack is the best man with that rifle I have ever seen anywhere, and he's accurate, never misses. I have a powerful hunch you two will be a force to reckon with in the future."

Jericho agreed with Harmon's assessment. He also felt the same kind of chemistry when they met today. But he ended their conversation by saying, "I don't want to hurt your feelings or deter your hospitality, but I'm going to find a boarding house or someplace with a softer bed. I couldn't abide that cell bunk another minute!" laughed Jericho and said, "Captain, I can promise you this, we will get out of your hair at sunrise tomorrow."

Jericho headed for the door. Once out on the porch, he began thinking, as he headed for the stables, that it would take a while to get used to calling his new deputy, Cactus Jack.

CHAPTER EIGHT

After sunrise and having a hearty breakfast later, Jericho walked out of the boarding house door to see the morning's weather. However, he was greeted with dark gray skies. Rain clouds remained, but off to the south, he could see a break as the sun desperately tried to shine through a veil of gloom.

He mumbled to himself; he should be thankful that the main force of the storm had passed, and the town was enveloped in a soft misty rain at the moment; it wouldn't dampen his spirits today. He mused. *Half of his intended goals had been met with the hiring of Jack.*

He stepped off the porch of the boarding house into the muddy streets and headed for Captain Harmon's office. As he walked, he thought, *Harmon Office is the home of the terrible bedding accommodations.* He smiled and thought how smart he had been to go to the boarding house last night. He should be patting himself on the back for such a wise decision.

The bed was very comfortable, and the hot bath eased the aching shoulders before he retired. This morning's breakfast was excellent. The best part was that he wasn't stiff and sore when he got up today.

Jericho looked up from his thoughts and saw Jack emerge from the Ranger Station, where he waved a greeting to his new partner. He sloshed through several puddles and soon joined Jack near the steps to the Ranger Station. Jericho smiled and said, "Morning, Jack."

Jack smiled, and Jericho could see he was anxious to get started. However, Jericho needed to finish his readiness and told Jack, "Before we get started, I need to visit the General Store here in town for some supplies and different clothes. While I'm tending to that business, would you mind getting our horses saddled?"

"Sure thing," answered Jack, "What kind of horse do you ride?" Jericho smiled and said, "When you get to the Livery, just ask the Hosteler which horse is mine. I'm sure he'll remember me. I threatened him with bodily harm, but I also paid him quite a bit of extra money for special care for my horse. Just ask the owner for a horse called Brutus; he'll recognize the name."

Don't worry about supplies, Jack answered, "I've got most everything together that I think we need; I'll be ready to ride when you are." Jack headed for the stables.

Jericho stepped off the boardwalk_into the mud-infested street and asked Jack, "Can you think of anything we might need for the trip while I'm at the General Store?"

"No, no, we're good; I think I've got a handle on everything we'll need for several days," replied Jack, "and everything else we can buy or kill along the way."

Jericho removed his saddlebags, threw them over his shoulder, and entered the general store. He purchased two pairs of jeans, three cotton shirts, a set of chaps, and a black plains duster. He treated himself to a new black rain slicker and a black Stetson hat. He took one pair of jeans and one of the new shirts into the store's back room and changed from his uniform into his new clothes.

Emerging from the back of the store, Jericho asked the clerk for paper and pen. Taking the pen in hand, he wrote a note to the Commanding Officer at the Garrison in Houston with his instructions for handling the Army's Equipment.

Jericho placed the note atop the folded uniform, telling the clerk, "These are items that belonged to the Army, and I want to return them as soon as possible." He asked if the clerk would place the note and clothes together with wrapping paper and heavy twine. Folding the duster and the rest of the new clothes and packing them into his saddle bags, he donned the new hat and slicker and left the store. Jericho carried the bundle under his arm, draped his saddlebags over his shoulder, and proceeded to the Ranger Station Office.

Once inside the office, Jericho placed the package on the captain's desk. "What's in the package?" asked the captain.

"It contains my uniform and some other items I need to return to the Garrison in Houston." Jericho asked Harmon, "I would appreciate it if you would ensure my package got out on the next stage and have the stage driver deliver it to the Orderly on Duty at the Post. He's to tell the Orderly that the package must be given to the Commander of the Garrison and him only. Jericho stated, "The Commander there knows I'm not returning to the post, and I explained everything in the letter of what I want done with its contents."

Jericho thanked Captain Harmon for all his assistance. They shook hands, and he wished the captain a quick recovery and good luck.

Jericho walked out the office door to find Jack sitting on his horse, holding on to his horse's reins. Nodding his thanks, Jericho threw his saddlebags over his horse's back and mounted.

He and Jack rode out of the town of Lufkin into the miserable, misty rain. For the first few miles, Jericho was a little unhappy with himself. He was starting their trip later than he would have liked, but shaking his head, he knew the delays were his own.

He set himself and took the lead, heading his horse in a southwesterly bearing. Following close behind, he pushed his horse to a trot to bring himself alongside Jericho.

Jack asked, "Where's your uniform? Shouldn't we be headed more to the northwest than the south?"

Jericho grinned at Jack, saying, "First of all, I stick out in a crowd in my uniform. And where we're going, I don't want to call attention to myself. Besides that, I'm no longer in the Army as of yesterday."

Jack shrugged. He didn't get the expected answer, so he took his beat-up old Stetson off to dump the water, shook the hat, and placed it back on his head. Jack hunched over against the wind and set himself against the persistent mist, which had become slightly heavier since they had left.

Looking skyward through the rain, Jack could see what appeared to be a break in the clouds further south. It gave him hope that their continued path to the southwest would eventually ride out the rain. Jack would welcome the warming rays of a mid-afternoon sun. Anything but this crappy rain would be a blessed relief.

Jericho began skirting the quagmire of the main roads to outdistance and dodging the puddles that were now fast filling over. He continued riding further south and set a course to follow the river road.

Both men quickly noticed that the river, which should typically be low at this time of year, had become a foaming, roiling mass of water.

Jericho knew that if the wet weather continued, it would be a major flooding problem for the area. Jericho was well aware of the soggy, sodden earth they were traversing. The mud was sucking at the horse's hooves and legs, and their mounts struggled to move without stumbling. Waving Jack to follow, Jericho urged his horse onto a small knoll. Several trees clustered together to form a small canopy, providing a haven from the rain for both men and their horses for a spell.

Jericho used his time to clean as much mud and grime from the horse's legs and hooves as possible. Jack also began cleaning his horse's hooves when he discovered a large stone in one of his left-back hoof. The horse had been lucky; under normal circumstances, a stone that large would have made his horse limp or crippled him. The soft earth they had been traveling on had kept the rock from harming the soft inner frog of his horse's hoof.

Jack had finished his wiping ministrations for a moment and had cleaned most of the mud from his horse.

But something was troubling Jack.

Jack cleared his throat to get Jericho's attention and said, "I'm not usually this nosey, but when I asked you before about your uniform and the change in clothes, I understood your reasoning. Jack continued, "But boss, you didn't answer my other question? Why are we going so far out of our way if we're supposed to be heading northwest toward Lubbock? Last time I heard tell, your Fort was up near there."

The question made Jericho pause, and he stopped momentarily to wipe the rain from his eyes and face with his bandana, and he figured it was time to answer Jack's question. But he stalled the conversation momentarily, thinking how he would respond. He bent over, renewing his rubbing the circulation back into his horse's legs while thinking about his response.

Finally, Jericho stopped rubbing and stood up, leaning on his horse. He said, "I didn't mention this before back at the Ranger Station when I first met you. I didn't even tell Captain Harmon, but I had two reasons for coming to this area of the State. The first reason you already know is finding you to take the new marshal's position. The second reason is that I've been tracking a gang of killers who robbed Fort Justice's payroll several weeks back. During the robbery, the gang killed all but one of the troopers. These men were under my command while escorting the payroll to the Fort. The men that were killed were soldiers I selected for that assignment." "And I feel an obligation to find the persons responsible for their deaths."

Jericho stopped a moment as he remembered his sorrow at losing his soldiers. It still burdened his heart, but he continued, "One soldier who survived, Corporal Finley, was the Non-Com in charge. He was severely wounded, but he managed to stay alive while the robbers were killing everyone else. His life was spared when another one of my soldiers that was killed had fallen across his body. It was Finley's good fortune that the gang didn't bother to check on the dead, and they rode off assuming they'd killed everyone.

Corporal Finley managed to make it back to the Fort alive. Although severely wounded, Finley recovered and told me his story while I visited him in the infirmary. He told me he recognized two gang members. These were men he had known long before he joined the Army. They were the twin boys of a family named Colbert. The Corporal had lived in the same area where the family had a ranch, and their homestead was just outside a town called Crocket. He thought the two boys' names were Brad and Jim Bob Colbert. He said they always raised hell when he knew of the family years before. He didn't recognize any of the others because his view was restricted by a dead body lying on him."

He did hear one of the twins yell out the name Zeke. He thought that Zeke might be the younger brother of Brad and Jim Bob."

Jericho paused before continuing, " I've been searching for the gang for quite some time. I've been traveling by train and horse these past few weeks trying to put together leads to their whereabouts. While on my way to a place where I could catch a train last week, I got a real lead to their location."

"I got a tip from a gal in a traveling Circus of all things. I met her in a saloon in the town where I could catch my train. I was lonely, and she was a good-looking filly. She and I became very friendly!"

CHAPTER NINE

Jericho didn't elaborate to Jack on what he meant by being *very friendly* as he continued. "The Circus was performing just outside of a place called Marabee Junction. The town was one of the whistle stops the Circus made yearly."

Jericho looked over at Jack, who had a scowl on his face. However, Jericho dismissed it and continued telling Jack about the tip.

"I had decided to stop at Marabee to get some supplies and catch the train later that night. At the same time, I saw a poster about the Circus being in town and decided to see the show. I caught the show's last act, and while I watched, it dawned on me the Circus would travel over the state. Someone might have seen or recognized the Colbert boys."

"I followed some performers who said they were headed for the local tavern. This gal was also in the group, and I watched her for a while. Later, I approached her and bought her a drink.

While drinking with her, I asked if she might have seen or heard of the Colbert gang."

I showed her the Wanted Poster of Brad Colbert, and he was wanted for the murder of a farmer from down around Freesburg. That's when she thought she recognized the man in the drawing. Jericho smiled at the memory and added, "Amanda was this gal's name. She told me that while the circus was performing in Crocket, the man she met was called Brad. He approached her after the show and wanted her to drink with him. She figured why not, and she accepted the invitation."

Then she began to describe Brad, saying, "This Brad fellow bragged about his prowess as a gunfighter and how he had come into a lot of money. He kept going on about some guy named Chester Adkins."

"Brad told her this guy Adkins was some genius for making money. Chester had hired him and some of his family to do a job for him to make them all rich."

"It was then that Amanda got a bad feeling about Brad and decided he was someone she didn't want anything to do with. She made up some excuse about having to help pack up because the Circus was getting ready to go to another town that night."

"That was a week ago yesterday that I talked with her." Jericho looked over his saddle at Jack, saying, "That's why I thought we'd make a little detour and swing south to check out the town. I want to see if there were more Colbert sightings around Crocket before going to the Fort, and I want to get these guys behind bars. They killed some fine troupers, and I swear I won't rest until I have them locked up."

Jericho looked at Jack, checking his response to his tale about the robbery.

Jack was deep in thought about something.

"Jack, what's troubling you so much?" asked Jericho.

Jack looked up with a frown. "I know something about them, boys. I've played poker with their dad many times before he died. I've even had supper with the whole family once or twice when the wife was still alive. I got the news sometime later that Brad Colbert had become the self-appointed boss of the family since their dad died. He fancies himself some badass with a gun, a tough hombre. I saw the handbill yesterday in our office, just before I met you. It must have been posted at the Ranger Station that day."

Jericho looked worried but asked, "Do you have a problem going after these people you once knew?"

Jack indignantly replied, "Not one bit. They aren't my friends. I was a friend of their dad and mom, and I didn't know much about the boys until later. Now that I know what they've done, helping you put them somewhere they can't harm anyone will be a pleasure. But if we're going to Crocket, I should warn you; the town has a crooked sheriff. His name is Hawkins. He's a real shady character, a real asshole, and a tough person to deal with, to boot."

"If the truth were known, I'll bet he's known that the Colberts were around all this time. I wouldn't put it past him to look the other way. He's probably getting paid on the side to ignore any wanted poster or trouble those boys might have caused."

Jericho mounted his horse but held it in check as he pondered the information that Jack had gathered. Armed with this new revelation, he concluded he was on the right track. He gigged his horse forward into a canter.

Jericho was now really anxious to get to the town of Crocket. He wanted to ask around about the Colberts while finding a place where they could rest the horses and themselves for the night.

Jack urged his horse to bring him alongside Jericho, and he could see that his information about the Colberts had Jericho excited. Jack was happy he could quickly add something of value to their new association. He was ready and willing to help Jericho find the killers he was so desperate to put behind bars.

Jericho lapsed into deep thought. He couldn't imagine his good luck. His deputy had provided a new lead, a hot possibility. For the first time, he looked closely at Jack and his horse. He couldn't help but notice the fluid grace of the horse and horseman riding beside him.

His attention focused on Jack's horse. Jack was riding one of the largest and most beautiful Appaloosa horses Jericho had ever seen. He had to admire how the Appaloosa seemed to have weathered the sloppy conditions relatively well, especially while supporting its huge rider throughout the morning's trek through the mud. Jericho concluded that Jack, sitting on his horse, was an imposing sight, one giant riding another giant.

Jack glanced over to Jericho, who seemed to have been eyeing him a long time, and asked, "Just what in the hell are you staring at me for? What did I do now?"

Jericho laughed. "I was just remembering that grip trick you tried on me. My hand still smarts from your handshake. But I was wondering, where did you get that monster of a horse you're riding?"

"It's quite a story and something I will never forget," replied Jack. "I broke this here horse about two years ago. It took me three tries, and she nearly broke me instead. While I was breaking her, she bruised and nearly crushed my balls while breaking her, and my balls were sore for a week from that fateful ride that day. While I was recovering, with me lying on my stomach, I wondered what I would call my horse. The name had to match her mean and ornery streak, and I settled on a name that seemed to fit my awful experience."

"Jericho, meet Cleo!" Jack smiled and doffed his hat at Jericho, saying, "Cleo, I want you to meet Jericho, my new partner."

Jack explained, "Cleo, that's short for Cleopatra. I heard somewhere about this gal named Cleopatra. It seems she was a queen in Egypt long ago, and I read that Cleopatra managed to bust several men's balls who were enchanted with her beauty. I figured this horse was the most beautiful thing I had ever seen, and the name seemed to fit."

Jack's face became serious, saying, "Cleo could match that queen anytime. Cleo knows how to bust a man's balls properly."

The rest of the ride became more of a search for detours to find better and more solid conditions for the horses so they wouldn't have to walk through the muddy quagmire and sloppy conditions. The two riders arrived in Crocket a little after sundown after two days of traveling on the sloppy roads of Texas.

Jack was happier now. Thankfully, the rain had finally stopped a while back. Because of overcast skies, the town was already engulfed in a shadowy gloom, and most of the porch lanterns were lit. They found the town's livery thanks to Jack's recalling its whereabouts. Once inside the stable, they stripped the saddles and blankets from their mounts.

Both men began rubbing down their horses with liniment. These men understood the importance of caring for their animals and ensured their horses' comfort before their own.

They also took extra time to apply the rubbing liniment ointment, which helped soothe and relieve the soreness and muscle cramps.

Jericho gave the Liveryman two dollars per horse for additional oats and warm blankets to reward their horse's fine work throughout the long ride. Jericho asked the Liveryman, "Where's the best eatery in Crocket?" The man suggested Roses Café.

Jack licked his lips and agreed, saying," I think I've eaten there before, and if it's the same place I remember, you get plenty of good food for your money." Jack and Jericho made their way to the Cafe, and both men chose the venison from the menu, which was delicious and filling. Afterward, when they had finished their fine meal, they ordered more coffee, and both men had a slice of homemade apple pie.

Jericho rubbed his belly and proclaimed, "That meal sure was fine; this place was a good choice." Smiling, Jericho arose and slapped Jack on the back as he quipped, "Eating sure has helped fill the void left where my ribs and backbone were rubbing together; it was making my insides nervous and uptight, with all the racket my bones were making." Jack couldn't help but smile. He knew he would have to sharpen his wits to keep up with his new boss because Jericho also had a sharp tongue.

"What we need now is some good whiskey to finish off our wonderful meal!" Jack suggested. "I know just the right place in this town that fills the bill."

Texas Belle Saloon is the best little saloon in these parts.

"Belle has the best whiskey for miles around! And she has the best-looking women anyone could hope for in a small town in the middle of nowhere Texas."

The two men left the cafe and headed down the street to the place that Jack had suggested. A few minutes later, Jericho followed Jack through the batwing doors of the Texas Belle's Saloon.

Standing just inside, Jericho heard, above the noise, two female voices squealing Jack's name. Two very fine-looking ladies detached themselves from the customers they were entertaining and rushed to Jack's side.

Each gal grabbed one of Jack's arms. Jack looked at both beauties and smiled as he pointed to each woman, saying, " This filly is Mary Lou patting the pretty dark-haired lady at his right arm, and the other lady on my left is the famous redheaded

Belle." Jack leaned over and kissed her cheek, adding, "And she owns this joint."

Jack grabbed Jericho's arm, pulling him forward to stand beside Belle. He then began the introductions, proclaiming, " This man is my new boss, Belle, and I hope you will treat him special." Jack smiled, telling Jericho about the ladies, and suggested, "Belle, why don't you take Jericho upstairs? Treat my boss with some of that good whiskey you keep hidden away, and please show him a really good time." Jack winked and again began smiling at something he was thinking. He finished his thoughts by saying, "In bed!"

Jericho just shook his head, thinking to himself, Jack, you're about as subtle as a fart in church, but he thought what the hell. Jack might have the right idea, and since he had nothing else planned and Belle was a lovely lady, he'd be a fool to pass up this opportunity.

Jericho tried to remember if Belle had said no to Jack's invitation, but as he looked at the enchanting beauty at his side, he quickly noticed. Belle had a death grip on his arm and didn't want to let go. Belle had the body that would make any man's heart jump for joy, and as Jericho looked into Belle's blue-green eyes, he quickly smiled at the vision before him.

Belle must have taken that as a sign that he approved what he saw and began guiding and pulling Jericho toward the stairs.

Jack, in the meantime, was looking across the room at the poker tables, and he unhooked his arm from Mary Lou, telling her, "I think I'll join that group of yokels playing poker and relieve them of their money."

Mary Lou yanked on Jack's arm, pouting, and complained, "Jack, you think more of them damn cards than you do of me."

Jack was quick to soothe his lady's unhappiness, telling her, "Mary Lou honey, please don't feel that way; I still want you and only you, and sweety, you're the love of my life, next to card playing, that is." But before heading for the poker tables, Jack looked down at Mary Lou and noticed she had tears in her eyes.

Jack reached around her with his big arms and brought her near to him, letting one of his hands rest on her ample buttocks. He patted her on the butt, saying, "Honey, don't look so sad; just give me a few minutes to fleece those local yokes, I need to unwind for a little while, and I promise I'll be along real soon."

Jack started to head for the card tables, but before he could move, Mary Lou grabbed his arm, spun him around, and kissed him, saying, "That's for luck, Cactus honey."

Jack pulled her tight to him again, almost crushing the wind from her, and gently kissed her lips again and told her, "Mary, you best be ready. It's not going to take me long at those poker tables. I'll sure be in the mood for some bedspring squashing romping high jinks."

Meanwhile, with Belle on his arm, Jericho had already left the smoky, crowded hall behind as they entered Belle's private rooms. Belle's apartment was immaculate and decorated to fit a queen. She told him to sit anywhere as she left his side to cross the room and opened the doors of a walnut cabinet against the wall.

Belle opened a cabinet and grabbed a bottle of her unique whiskey, the same whiskey Jack bragged about. She brought the amber-colored liquor to where Jericho had found a chair of his liking, one of Belle's beautiful and comfortable overstuffed chairs.

Belle removed the cork stopper, poured the brown-colored liquor into two glasses on the nearby table, and sat in the matching chair beside him. She handed him one of the glasses and took the other for herself. They touched their glasses together as a salute to their new friendship.

Belle quickly drank her whiskey in two gulps. Setting her glass aside, she stood up and unbuttoned her dress.

"Hurry up with that drink!" she demanded, "get out of those clothes, lover. I can hardly wait for us to be naked together."

Belle wasn't wasting any time; her clothes were flying off her body in record speed, and sashes, petticoats including her satin and lacey underclothes, were quickly on the floor, trailed in little piles as she walked to the enormous bed that took up a good portion of her apartment.

Jericho noticed with a smile that Belle was a true redhead, from top to bottom.

Belle turned and beckoned Jericho to join her as she sat down on the bed; her smile had that come-hither lusty look as she finished removing the last articles of clothing, her stockings, and her garter belt.

Jericho's breath came in quick gasps as he looked upon the beautiful naked woman.

Belle was a woman whose beauty he hadn't seen the equal to for a long while. With one gigantic gulp of his drink, Jericho set the glass on the table, stood up, and started to take off his clothing. However, he wasn't moving fast enough for her likes.

Belle stood up wholly naked and came quickly over to where Jericho was standing and began helping him remove his remaining clothing as fast as her fingers and thumbs would work. Once Jericho was as naked as Belle, she began tugging and pulling him toward the bed.

Jericho met her challenge, and he and Belle tumbled naked onto her bed, entwined in a fervent embrace.

Jericho gazed at the entire length of Belle's body and realized he was a lucky man indeed. Belle was blessed with large breasts with large puffy nipples, a rarity in most women. He caressed and cupped one of her breasts as her nipple began to harden in his hand. He bent down and brought his mouth down upon her breast, taking the nipple into his mouth, all the while the other hand caressed her other breast.

A gasp and a long moan signaled her pleasure, and she grasped Jericho's head, pushing his face harder into her ample chest.

Jericho snaked a hand down her body to between her legs to fondle and strum the little button at the beginning of_her inner core. Belle began to wither in ecstasy as she moaned incoherent whispered pleas, but Belle's hand was also busy as she grasped his manhood in a vicelike grip, stroking him up and down into a fiery frenzy.

When his ardor had reached its limits, and he was as hard as a rock, he raised himself over her into a position between her legs so he could enter her steaming wet womanhood. Belle's breath came in gasps as she begged him to hurry. She couldn't wait for another second, and Jericho answered her pleas as he sank into her heated, slick, volcanic core.

Jericho's massive root was completely seated.

The two of them were fused for a long moment, savoring the combination of their fiery heat. Then, she encouraged Jericho to go deeper into her inner core.

Once he reached her core's limits, it was as if her depths were grasping him like a hard handshake. He, in turn, began pulling back until only the tip remained at her inner entrance and then sank back down into her depths, again and again, faster and faster. He began to repeat this motion until Belle cried out her earth-shattering release as her fluids gushed around his manhood. Jericho's powerful release was seconds behind Belle's as she collapsed onto his chest in utter bliss.

Several minutes of quiet euphoria passed between them. Then Belle raised and kissed him passionately, running her tongue between his lips. She focused her eyes to meet Jericho's eyes, smiled, and whispered, "Thank you for that wonderful experience; I am still tingling, but I hope there is much more to come, lover."

Jericho noticed a fine layer of moisture on her face from their fiery passion, but he also saw a contented woman.

Belle got up moments later and disappeared into her bathroom. She returned with a towel and bent down and wiped Jericho's face and chest, then down between his hips to his semi-hard manhood. Jericho reached his arms to hold her, but Belle had other ideas. She bent down and licked his nipple and quickly moved down to run her tongue in his navel, and before he could protest, she engulfed the tip of his manhood with her mouth.

Jericho almost jumped out of his skin, and her mouth was as heated as her core.

His manhood reacted immediately when she took his rod entirely into her mouth, and just like a feat of magic, he became hard as a rock again, languishing in the intense feeling of pleasure, and it was his turn to gasp.

Just when he thought he couldn't last much longer, Belle released his manhood from her mouth, raised, and straddled his body until she was poised above his hard stalk, grabbed his manhood, and guided him once again into her overheated core.

She smiled at Jericho, saying, "You should last much longer this time, lover. I want it slow and sensual, honey. It's been a long time since I had something this big in me, and I want to savor the feeling as long as possible."

And to Jericho's delight and good fortune, Belle proved to be quite adept at the art of lovemaking. Belle could control her inner muscles at her core, which gripped and milked his manhood to the utmost.

That good time Jack had asked her to provide became a reality, and Belle provided much more than he ever had anticipated. Belle tested Jericho's stamina and determination as she entertained and delighted him beyond his wildest dreams or imagination. Finally, their incredible lovemaking came to a joyful end in a mutual explosion of their desires, and they were fulfilled in a shattering climax.

And for the time being, for now, anyway, he savored the blissful afterglow of her tremendous and passionate bliss. For the first time in days, Jericho was thoroughly relaxed. He half-rolled onto his side, grabbed several pillows, and propped them under his head.

This position allowed him to enjoy the incredible beauty of the woman visibly stretched out before him. His fingers began lightly drawing circles through Belle's red curly tresses as she lay on her back, her beauty in full display.

Jericho couldn't believe his good fortune; he had tasted her great liquor, he had enjoyed her great body twice, and the night was still young.

Belle was a marvel, a lady that most men would never enjoy, and he knew he had been treated to something and someone special. Jericho clasped Belle in his arms and rolled together until Belle was nestled in the crook of his arm.

Jericho was curious and asked Belle, "Do you have a first name? Is Belle your family name?"

Belle smiled and looked up at him, saying, "No, honey. My given name is Belinda Munford, but Jericho, don't you dare tell anyone. I prefer being called Belle to my friends, and you, my dear, are certainly one of my newest best friends."

Belle rolled onto her side, facing him; she propped herself up with her elbow as her green eyes looked him over lustily. And she smiled, saying, "Big man, you're about the prettiest and sexiest man I have ever had the pleasure of sharing my bed with for as long as I can remember. I want you to know I don't make it a habit to have sex with my patrons, but when I first saw you, I had to have you, and you proved to be one hell of a lover."

"Darling, I ain't going to charge you for those wonderful romps in the hay or for the whiskey you drank, but just so you know, honey, if you ever come through Crocket again and you don't make an effort to see me, I'll cut that large instrument of pleasure from your body."

As her devilish demeanor changed, she smiled and said, "My whiskey, bed, and body will always be free to you, handsome."

Jericho thought to himself that he should take her warning seriously. Belle looked like a woman used to having her way, and Jericho was sure that no man would ever cross her on purpose, or there would be hell to pay if he did.

His thoughts were interrupted when Belle began playing with his shrunken manhood; as her mouth came close for another kiss, she extended her tongue playfully, licking his lips. It was a blatant invitation for Jericho to continue their lovemaking, and as she reached for him, all the shooting and hollering started.

CHAPTER TEN

Jericho quickly found his pants and tried to hurry to put them on. He found his shirt but left it open; he was too busy to stop and fasten all the buttons.

Colt in hand, he charged barefoot through the door to the hall to see what was happening. Jericho took a quick peek over the railing and had a clear view of what was going on the floor below. His immediate thoughts were that the scene before him was nothing less than chaotic.

Jericho's attention was drawn to the body of a man sprawled on the floor by the batwing doors, and Jack was standing by a chair next to the poker table with his smoking gun in his hand.

Jack was focused on the two other men standing just inside the batwing doors right next to the body.

Jack yelled, "You Colbert boys are as stupid as when I knew you as kids. Christ almighty!" Jack cursed again, "Damnit, all to hell. I told your brother Brad that he was under arrest, and I gave him a fair chance to surrender, but him being the dam fool that he was, he thought he could shoot his way out of all his problems."

Jack's voice boomed louder, "Brad and you both heard me when I told you to put your hands high. His actions proved to me how stupid men can sometimes be, and now he's the one that's dead."

Jack pointed to the star on his chest and said to the other two men, "I'm a sworn officer of the law, a ranger of the state of Texas. Your brother Brad was a wanted man for murdering some farmer down in the town of Freeburg. I had no choice but to take him in, and I would have seen that he got a fair trial."

Jack continued his warning, growling, "I'm telling you both, don't you two go and do something crazy. Keep your hands away from your guns; I want to talk to you both about a payroll robbery a while back."

Meanwhile, Jericho was delighted. What a stroke of luck. They'd come to the town of Crocket on the slight chance of finding the Colbert gang's trail, and here today, the Colberts were in Belle's Saloon; it was fate itself. The Colbert gang had found them.

Jericho watched Jack put his gun back in his holster, then leaned on the table and focused his full attention on the two men.

However, Jericho could see that Jack was becoming more agitated and angrier, but looking at the two men, they seemed unaware of their situation.

"I told you both, and I won't repeat it!" barked Jack, "unfasten those gun belts and drop them to the floor before I'm forced to put holes in you both."

Jericho was about to tell Jack he was above him, but he had to eat his words when one of Colbert's boys ignored Jack's warnings and foolishly reached for his gun to challenge him.

Jack's gun was holstered, and he was leaning on the poker table. It seemed to Jericho that the fool about to draw on Jack and Jack wasn't paying attention.

That's when the brother decided his fate yelling his challenge, "God damn you, Jack," the brother cried, you killed my brother Brad! No man does that and lives to tell about it as long as I'm alive." He snaked his hand down to the gun on his hip as he started to draw his weapon."

Jericho held his tongue. It was the wrong time for him to distract Jack.

Zeke had pulled his gun, and it had just cleared its holster and managed to point it in the direction of Jack, but before he could bring his weapon to bear entirely or fire, Jack's hand, in one quick, fluid, and continuous motion, drew and shot another Colbert brother.

The man known as Zeke Colbert was a dead man standing. His body hadn't yet told his brain that the bullet had pierced his chest and gone through his heart, as his body slumped to the floor dead.

Jack was quick to react and leveled his gun to cover the remaining man standing and demanded, "Jim Bob, drop your gun belt to the floor, and do it now. Don't you be a fool like your brothers; don't make a move; I don't want to kill you, too."

Jack fired a warning slug into the floor near Jim Bob to emphasize what he had been saying. "This whole mess has gone far enough; I'm getting a little sick and tired of killing the men in the Colbert family."

Jim Bob was the last of the Colbert family alive, but he wasn't any smarter than the rest of his family. He cried out, "I thought we knew you, Jack Harden! My Brothers and I thought you were our friend, and I remember you even visited our dad occasionally, and we sat together for meals."

"Now you've gone and killed all my brothers, damn you to hell, Jack, you've killed my whole family right in front of me. You're a no-good son-of-a-bitch." And like the fool that he was, he drew his gun and brought it up to point at Jack.

Jim Bob was faster on the draw than his brothers, but the bullet went wild in his hurry.

The slug missed Jack and plowed into a post beside his shoulder.

Jericho was astonished as he witnessed Jack standing without fear; the slug from Jim Bob's gun didn't even make him flinch.

Jack fired his gun twice, hitting Jim Bob squarely, one slug in his gut and the other slug dead center of his forehead.

Jericho yelled and got Jack's attention in time for him to look up. Thinking that the fight was over, Jericho started down the stairs.

However, a roar from the right of the steps immediately alerted Jericho to the two men firing from the balcony.

Jericho turned half around. Looking up, he saw two men firing weapons at Jack. Jack just stood firm through the withering fire as the two men were firing their guns down upon his partner.

Jericho drew quickly as he brought his gun to bear and fired at the nearest shooter. His bullet hit the man dead center, right between his eyes. Jericho swung his weapon upon the other gunman but had to hold his fire. The remaining shooter had grabbed one of the girls who had strayed from one of the rooms.

The man held her as a shield, firing around her at Jericho. Two deadly shots were dispatched in the direction of where Jericho was standing. One of the bullets hit the stairs in front of Jericho, while another grazed his gun hand, forcing him to let go of his weapon, which clattered down the steps below.

Jericho quickly flattened himself behind one of the rail posts, hoping it would provide some shelter.

Thankfully for Jericho, the girl the gunman was holding managed to twist away from the man's grip, and that move helped to throw the man's aim off. His next shot went into the ceiling. This whole episode played out in just mini-seconds, and now that the gunman was completely clear of the girl, he righted himself. Jericho was a sitting duck and entirely at the mercy of the man, and as the gunman leveled his gun at Jericho for a kill shot, in that split second, Jericho knew he would be too late to get out of the way or retrieve his weapon.

He heard the roar of a weapon and instinctually ducked his head, then he realized he felt no pain.

Looking up, Jericho was a bit puzzled, and then he saw the gunman drop his gun from his lifeless hand as he pitched forward over the rail of the landing, tumbling headlong onto the floor below.

Jack Harden blew the smoke from the end of his gun, grinning as he looked up toward Jericho, who stood and yelled, "Hey boss, glad you could join me! Is this what you had in mind when you said my job would be to cover your ass?"

Jericho smiled, yelling at his deputy, "Thanks for saving my bacon; I owe you one."

Jack began clearing his Remington 44. He removed the spent cylinder from the gun, placed the empty cylinder in his belt, took a new cylinder from the belt, and put it in the Remington.

Jericho was sure the shooting was over. He returned to Belle's apartment to complete his dressing. While dressing, he told Belle what had happened, took her in his arms, and kissed her hard. Then, he hurried off to join Jack.

Jericho stooped down and picked up his gun from the stairs. As he went down the stairs, his hand still smarted from the bullet strike. Then, he carefully checked to see if there was any damage to the gun's working mechanism. Nothing seemed wrong, and he continued down the staircase. He was three steps from the bottom when the batwing doors flew open, and in walked a grizzly old man wearing a silver badge, shotgun in hand.

Jericho froze in his tracks, and then he surmised this had to be the Town's Sheriff, the very one Jack had warned him about. And the sheriff had the shotgun out in front of him, pointed at the middle of Jack's chest.

The old sheriff fixed a glare upon Jack and growled, "Damn you, Jack Harden. Whenever you come near my town, I must tend to the wounded or bury somebody." The sheriff became belligerent, demanding, "Jack, now tell me, just what lame excuse do you have for killing all those Colbert boys?"

The old man pointed to all the bodies lying around and said, "I see you also managed to kill Colbert's cousins, Mike and Wayne Hargrove, too."

Angrily Jack responded in kind, "Hawkins, you're a walking disgrace to this town and a piss poor excuse for a man or sheriff on top of that." Jack continued with disdain, "You had to know the Colbert gang was here in town, and you had to know that Brad Colbert was wanted, and you did nothing about it."

In retort, the old sheriff haughtily spoke, "Look here, Jack, need I remind you; I'm the boss around here, and I don't recognize your authority in my town; you can take your slanderous remarks about me and your shitty attitude and get the hell out of here.

Better yet, I think I'll let you cool your heels in my jail until I can get a judge to rule on these killings. Drop your gun belt, Jack. You're under arrest for all these killings tonight!"

Jericho assessed the situation and didn't like what he saw. Aiming carefully, he shot and hit the trigger housing of the shotgun.

His bullet had done precisely what Jericho had intended; it had first knocked the shotgun offline while rendering the gun useless, and the shotgun would not ever fire again.

CHAPTER ELEVEN

Jericho watched as the sheriff stumbled back. His face told the story; he was a dumbfounded man who couldn't grasp what had happened.

Jack seized the opportunity, stepping quickly to confront the sheriff. He was face to face with the startled sheriff in the blink of an eye. Jack grabbed the greener out of the sheriff's grip and threw it to land near the front wall of the bar. Grabbing the sheriff's shirtfront with one of his giant fists, he began twisting and knotting the shirt into a tight ball. Jericho could see the ball was so tight that it was causing the sheriff to turn red from a lack of air.

Jack brought his fist and the sheriff level with his face, which also meant the sheriff's body was a foot off the floor. Sheriff Hawkins was about to pass out. He couldn't move, and his breath was cut off.

Jericho noticed that no one protested or came to the sheriff's defense; no one would help the sheriff from this room. Jericho surmised the sheriff had managed to piss off almost everyone in the town.

Glaring with eyes afire, Jack began shaking the old sheriff like a rag doll until he noticed Hawkins's eyes rolling back into his head. Jack took pity and relaxed his arm to allow the sheriff's feet to touch the floor. He loosened his grip on the sheriff's shirt to allow him to breathe, but he didn't let go. He still held the knotted shirt while he growled into the face of the sheriff as he stated, "Hawkins, I've had all the crap I can stand from you. You and I both know a Ranger, any Ranger in Texas, has all the authority they need in this town or any town in the State to make arrests! I'm just the man who's going to send your ass packing off to your jail."

Jack pushed the sheriff into a chair. He looked around the room until he found who he was looking for. The man Jack was seeking stood riveted near the bar rail, and Jack called out to him, saying, "Mr. Mayor, your town needs a new sheriff! Hawkins has just proven to me that he's heavily involved with those dead men. He's been harboring criminals and using his office to look the other way when crimes have been committed.

I'm making him a guest of his jail just as soon as I can arrange his transport."

Jack looked over the crowd, seeking someone, but didn't see that person in the bar. He called to the mayor, saying, " Go find Duane Johnson for me. I know he's been a deputy off and on for several years, so get him here as fast as you can." Jericho watched as the mayor hurried out the bar's doors into the night.

Several minutes passed, and surprisingly, the room remained calm.

Jericho stood rooted to his spot on the stairs and marveled in awe at his new deputy's work. Jack was in full command of the room and didn't need him to interfere.

A little while later, the batwing's doors swung open, and the man Jack had asked to see walked in. Jack called to him and said, "Duane, Duane Johnson! Damnit, man, step to it and get your ass on over here."

Duane Johnson looked bewildered and looked at Jack for a moment. Then he did as he was told and hurried to where Jack stood.

Jack put his arm around Duane's shoulder and pointed to the old sheriff, who was sitting and still shaking. He said,

"Duane, I believe you've been a part-time deputy for the town, haven't you?" Duane was not surprised by the question. Jack assumed the mayor had told him about the commotion at the bar. Duane seemed hesitant but finally answered Jack, saying, " Yes, sir, I've been a deputy a few times these past few years."

Jack's face took on a serious look as he took Duane's hand and began shaking it, saying, "I'm appointing you to be the temporary sheriff; I've just arrested ole man Hawkins for a bunch of crimes." Jack reached down and yanked the old man from the chair, shoved him in front of Duane, and said, "Duane, I think you're just the man who can handle the job as the sheriff. I hope you'll accept the full-time job, but for now, it's as a temporary sheriff."

Duane nodded, and his demeanor changed suddenly. His body became more erect, and his shoulders squared as he proclaimed, "You bet Jack, I mean Ranger Harden. I'll take the job, and you can count on me. However, Duane looked puzzled and asked, "What do you want done? I have never had this much responsibility before."

Jack momentarily focused on the beleaguered old sheriff and looked back at Duane, telling him, "Don't worry about what is expected tonight. Just get him into a cell at the jail. I'll come by in the morning, and we'll talk long about duties."

Jack seemed pleased with all that had transpired as he began getting ready for the exchange of sheriffs. He then started reciting some of the words of the oath of office. Jericho had to smile at Jack's_mangled version of the oath of the Office of Sheriff; it was probably the first time Jack had ever had to say the words.

Jack's hand reached over to where the sheriff was standing and ripped the badge attached to the old man's vest, as he explained to Duane, saying, "This badge and my words make the job official. He then pinned the badge on Duane's shirt front."

Turning to the crowd, Jack proclaimed, "Duane is your town's new sheriff. You can keep Duane as sheriff or vote for somebody else when the time comes."

Then turning back to the new sheriff, Jack told Duane, "Your first official act as the new sheriff is to take this piece of shit Hawkins and put him behind bars. I'll come by first thing tomorrow with my new boss, pointing to Judge Starr. I will soon be his new deputy, but I am still a Ranger and a sworn Officer of the State of Texas. I'll have Judge Starr make out papers sending this garbage to the Territorial Prison for a long time."

"Duane, do you need help transporting Hawkins?" questioned Jack.

"There won't be any problems, Jack!" Duane answered, pushing the old sheriff through the bar's doors on their way to the town jail.

Jericho stood looking down at all the carnage in the room. It was all centered around Jack, and he thought his instincts about Jack were confirmed. Jack Harden was the right man for the job, indeed.

Jack saw Jericho standing on the stairs, smiled, and motioned for him to come down and join him.

Jericho took Jack aside and began discussing the points of law that would probably cover the crimes that Hawkins had perpetrated. They also discussed some of the finer points of Jack's oath of office speech. Jericho slapped Jack on the back of the soon-to-be deputy and told him he would re-swear the oath when they went to jail in the morning.

The rest of that night for both men was anything but boring.

Mary Lou was standing at the bar and immediately had a death grip on Jack's arm. Jericho surmised Jack would fulfill those promises he'd made to her before the shootings had begun earlier. Soon after, Jericho and Jack parted to join their respective ladies.

Jericho entered Belle's apartment, and she stood majestically in full display. She had on an exotic floral night robe, the color that highlighted her beautiful red tresses.

Delightfully, his expectations became reality as Belle removed the robe, and Jericho could see that Belle was gloriously naked under the robe.

Looking flustered, she stood with her hands on her hips, then demanded, "Get those damn clothes off, honey! What the hell are you waiting for?"

Belle turned, let the night robe drop off her shoulders, and jumped on the bed naked. However, there was no way that Jericho was that fast. And it took him several minutes before he also joined her naked in the bed.

Jericho was more than ready to revisit the woman's lovely body next to him. The two lovers kissed and hugged passionately in a loving embrace, about to renew what had happened earlier.

They were rudely interrupted by loud shouts and moaning, and then they began to hear the bed squeaking, banging, and thumping.

The noise had to be coming from Mary Lou's room.

Jericho and Belle stopped, sat up, and looked at each other; Belle broke the mood of their moment when she looked at Jericho, grinned, and complained, "I'm sorry, lover, but I can't concentrate with all those noises and hollering going on."

Jericho couldn't help himself as he laughed at the preposterous situation and said to his bedmate, "I am going to have nightmares just thinking about ole Jack and his thunderous lovemaking."

"I don't know whether to feel sorry for me or feel happy for Mary Lou. After all, she's having the time of her life, and I have to lay here and listen."

CHAPTER TWELVE

"Get up," yelled Jericho as he banged Mary Lou's door. Jack, I think we've got a big problem!"

Far off in his foggy mind, Jack heard a loud and continuous noise that was trying to awaken the big man from his stupor. Jack finally recognized where the loud noise was emanating from. It was Jericho's voice, and he was the one constantly banging on the door. Jack desperately tried to comply with the voice's commands. He swung his legs off the right side of the bed and tried to sit up, but his first effort failed miserably as he fell back onto the rumpled bed. He tried again, but this time, he could only get to a semi-upright position before the room began to spin out of control. He was forced to close his eyes and fall back onto the bed, flinging his arm wide to stop the bed from spinning.

The third try was finally successful, and after several deep breaths, he renewed his effort to sit up and yelled back at the voice on the other side of the door, "I hear you, I hear you. Quit your yelling and stop that insistent banging noise. I'm coming."

Putting both feet on the cold floor, Jack bent his body forward enough to ease the headache and sickness in his stomach. He sat with elbows on his knees and hands clasped tightly on either side of his head, trying to ease the pain and the ache in his stomach. Try as he might, the sickness in his stomach roiled enough to bring the bile upward into his throat.

Jack had no one to blame; too much whiskey, too little sleep, and too much excitement from the night before were just a few of the things that came to mind.

Meanwhile, Mary Lou began to stir from all the racket. She grabbed a large pillow and put it over her head to muffle the noise. Her efforts also exposed her beautiful derriere, which didn't go unnoticed by Jack as he gently patted and rubbed the two ample butt cheeks.

Jack finally stood up and looked down at his beautiful bedmate, remembering last night's bliss with the lovely lady. Jack gathered his senses and began struggling into his clothes. He found one of his boots under the bed and pulled the leather boot over his cold foot. Glancing around, he finally found the other boot hidden under the covers lying on the floor.

Patting the naked buttocks again didn't seem to faze the snoring Mary Lou, who hadn't moved a muscle through all of Jack's ministrations.

Jack finished dressing by strapping on his gun belt and doffing his hat. He had finished preparing himself enough to meet whatever Jericho was trying to tell him through the door.

When Jack opened the door, he was met by a scowl and a troubled expression on Jericho's face. Jericho began explaining the dire situation, and whatever fogginess Jack felt vanished. His boss's words jolted Jack's senses into focus when he said, "Partner, we have to hurry. We both messed up last night."

Jericho couldn't wait any longer and grabbed Jack's arm. As he urged Jack into action, he pulled the big man along as they raced for the stairs to the lower level. As they went down the stairs, Jericho finished explaining. "Something was bothering me late last night, and a thought kept poking at the edges of my mind until it finally dawned on me."

"We told that whole crowd in that saloon last night that we were looking to question the Colbert's for a robbery. I'm sure somebody will be able to put two and two together and come up with the same idea I had early this morning. If the Colbert boys didn't have a lot of money when we searched through their clothes, where's the loot from the robbery?"

As the two men shouldered through the doors on a dead run, Jericho said, " Let's start by looking over at the Livery. I assume that Colbert's horses will probably be there. As I remember, they weren't tied outside Belle's place. Maybe their saddlebags will have the payroll stored in them?"

Jack was a step ahead of Jericho and grabbed the handle of one of the large doors. He began to swing it open, and they were greeted with two bullets being fired from the interior of the stables.

The shots buzzed so close that both men flattened themselves to the ground. Crawling on their bellies, they both did a crab crawl back behind the open door. Another shot rang out, and the flame and smoke from the sniper's pistol helped Jericho get a fix on the general direction of the shooter. The shooter was somewhere deep in the interior of the Livery, past the tack room, but somewhere neither lawman could see.

"Partner, we were both lucky just now," remarked Jericho. We made a mistake when we were highlighted against the early morning light. Being lucky is sometimes better than being good. Thankfully, we are not dead or wounded. Don't forget, the good Lord was also looking after us. And let's thank God the shooter is a lousy shot!" grimaced Jack.

Jericho stood up behind the door and called to the person who had fired the shots, "Throw down your gun; you can't escape. There's only one door out of here, and we both got that covered. However, his little speech only brought another shot and a reply from the shooter somewhere in the interior of the Livery.

"I got nothing to lose now that you're here. Come get your helping of lead if you want me that bad."

Jericho squatted down to where Jack lay on his side and said in a low voice, "I remember seeing a window around the side of the Livery when we stabled our horse last night. Give me a couple of minutes and try to keep the shooter busy while I get to the window."

Jericho left, and Jack began to count off the two minutes in his mind. And he rolled into position in front of the open door and started firing his Navy Colt into the blackness of the Livery. A heartbeat later, the shooter fired two more bullets near the space where Jack was lying.

Jack heard glass break and Jericho's voice demanding, "Don't move asshole! If you move, I'll have no choice but to shoot you, and I'm sure you won't like that outcome."

Jack stood up, peeked around the stable door, and cautiously entered the gloomy interior. Not knowing what the shooter was about to do, Jack continued slowly moving until he finally saw a man standing beside one of the stalls at the back of the livery. He had his hands above his head, a gun held loosely in his fingers. "Drop the gun now!" demanded Jack.

The man let the gun fall from his grasp, but he kept his arms in the air to show he was no threat. Jack recognized the man; he was one of the gamblers he had played poker with at the tables the previous night. Jack started toward the man, and he inadvertently stumbled over the older man who owned the Livery. He stooped down to see if the man was breathing. He rolled the older man over onto his back. Thankfully, he began to moan as his eyes fluttered open. Jack got his hands under the man's shoulders and brought him up to sit.

"What happened? How long have I been out?" groaned the old man.

"Don't rightly know," replied Jack. "We just got here ourselves." "I think we got the guy who put that gash in your head. As Jack pointed to the man with his hands in the air, he noticed the gambler had begun to lower his hands. "Mister, keep those hands in the air until I tell you different," warned Jack.

As Jericho entered the Livery's main door, he saw that Jack had everything in hand. He saw Jack pointing to the old man struggling to rise and said, "The old man got quite a bump on his head thanks to the joker over there."

Jack told Jericho, "He's the guy who's been trying to kill us." Jericho turned towards the man with his hands above his head. The man was looking sad and forlorn.

Jericho moved forward as he spoke to Jack, saying, " Keep him covered. I'll check him for hide-out weapons." Jericho frisked the gambler quickly but found nothing of consequence in the way of other weapons. 'You can put your hands down slowly." Jericho commanded, "Now tell me, who are you, mister?"

The gambler proceeded to lower his hands slowly. His face was a mask of worry, and he replied, "Most people call me Fast Eddie Cole."

"Fast Eddie, you just earned yourself some jail time for this little stunt you pulled today," remarked Jericho. "I'll be charging you for hitting an old defenseless man into unconsciousness. There'll be charges for trying to kill legally appointed Lawmen in the State of Texas. These crimes will get you plenty of cell time for your troubles."

"How was I supposed to know you two were lawmen?" Groaned the gambler.

"Don't make a difference who we are," Jack quickly added. "You tried to kill both of us without provocation and forethought."

The gambler blanched white and began to explain, "Please believe me, I didn't come to kill anyone. I was looking for the money from the robbery you talked about last night in the saloon. The old man surprised me, and I had to keep him quiet."

Jericho thought for a moment and then looked at the gambler. "Well, since you don't look like you have any money stuffed in your shirt or pockets, and I didn't find any money when I searched you, I assume you didn't find anything!"

"I looked through the horse's saddlebags belonging to them Colbert's," ventured the Gambler. "But I didn't find any money; I only found dirty laundry and half-eaten jerky. If those Colbert boys had money, it wasn't on their horses."

Jericho was fed up with Fast Eddie and asked, "Jack, would you take our would-be thief over to the jail, and while you're there, look in on our other prisoner, the old Sheriff?"

"I'll check out these saddlebags myself and be along as soon as possible."

CHAPTER THIRTEEN

A few minutes later, Jericho joined Jack at the Sheriff's office and began his first duties as a Judge. He began swearing out charges against Fast Eddie for assault. After he had finished that paperwork, he started making out the arrest warrant charging Sheriff Hawkins. The charges were harboring criminals, abetting a crime, and attempted murder of a Texas Ranger.

Jericho finished his remaining duty by reciting the proper oath of office to Duane.

With these duties completed, Jericho and Jack suggested that Duane hire a deputy as soon as possible. He would need someone to watch the jail and the town while he was away delivering the old sheriff to the Army Garrison in Houston. From there, the proper authorities would process and transport him to the Territorial Prison."

Jericho's brow had deep-set wrinkles. He was thinking about something that troubled him. He asked, "Duane, did you see anyone leaving Crocket who might be heading toward the Colbert's place this morning?"

Duane thought for a minute and replied, "Come to think of it, I did see three of the town's merchants headed out that way about an hour ago. Why do you want to know who's leaving town?" asked the new sheriff.

"It might be that someone else is worried about the money the Colberts stole, and they could be headed to their place," Jericho replied.

"Oh, before I forget, the old sheriff wants to talk with you, Jericho," remarked Duane. He's claiming he has information he wants to trade to help lessen his sentence; he sounds serious and says he knows about something big that will happen in Emerald City."

Jericho was puzzled thinking. *What in the hell does he think he has that would possibly lighten the charges against him?* With Jack beside him, Jericho left the office area and went to the cells in the back of the building.

Confronting the old sheriff, Jericho asked, "Ok, Hawkins, what vital information do you think you have?"

"You both have me all wrong," Hawkins stated, "I was just about to arrest those Colbert boys when Jack there, kilt the whole clan!"

"Cut the crap Hawkins." As anger crept into his voice, Jericho stated, "I don't believe you have any information that will change my mind or your sentence. I've wasted enough time with you as it is!"

"Wait, wait," the old sheriff begged. I know you're mad at me for all I've done."

"You should know what I know about a man in Emerald City," pleaded Hawkins. "There's a man named Chester Adkins there, and he's about to wage war on the Comanche Indian Tribe somewhere near the town. I was told they have quite a few cattle, and he will steal them soon. I overheard the Colbert brothers talking, and Brad had been told that this Adkins feller wants to erase those Indians from the face of this earth. He's got a small army of gunslingers ready to finish the job.

The old sheriff went on to say that this man called Adkins gave orders to kill everybody, including Indians, Settlers, and anybody who got in their way. He's also behind the killings of settlers and ranchers for their cattle and property in other places.

The old sheriff finished telling Jericho, "Adkins is the one who gave the Colbert's gang the information about the Fort's Payroll."

"I'll pass that information along, and I'll let the person I report to know that you helped with your information. If this proves true, you might have saved your hide from dying in prison. This information might be crucial to my superior. It should be something he will want to know."

Jericho mulled over what Hawkins had said. The sheriff's words had a special meaning for Jericho. Jericho was an honorary member of the Tribe that Adkins was trying to wipe away.

Leaving the Hawkins' cell and returning to the office, Jericho put that knowledge in the back of his mind for later.

He asked Duane, the new sheriff, "What can you tell me about those three men you saw riding out this morning?" Jericho explained his line of questions, adding, "I'm almost sure that those merchants are headed for the Colbert Ranch. They might be trying to see if the boys left stolen money around their place."

"Sheriff," Jack and I will go to Colbert's place. It would be a good idea to follow us out to the Colbert place as soon as you can find someone to watch your prisoners. I suggest you and the Livery owner share in selling the Colbert Clan's horses and gear. Their equipment should cover any costs owed to the Livery and the costs associated with boarding and feeding your new jail inhabitants."

The two Lawmen began their journey to the Colbert ranch as dark skies threatened rain.

Jack rode ahead, taking the lead, saying, "I know the way! And like I said before, I've often been to the Colbert ranch."

The ride was a short distance from the town.

Thirty minutes later, Jack stopped, waved Jericho to come alongside, pointed to where the road split off, and said, "Their cabin is about a half mile further up this road, maybe a hundred yards further atop that knoll on our left."

As the two men neared the ranch house, they dismounted and walked their horses to a grove of trees that would be good cover. Their spot provided a good view through the trees' foliage, but they were sure nobody from the cabin could see them.

From their vantage point, both men could see the front of the house. Three horses were tied to the hitching rail. Jericho and

Jack talked it over and agreed to split up. Jack would go around back, and Jericho would wait five minutes and then approach the front of the house.

Quietly, Jericho counted off five minutes and began creeping towards the front of the house. As he drew closer, he could hear noises and things being moved and knocked over inside the home.

He heard someone inside the house proclaim, "There's nothing here? We've checked these rooms several times, and they look empty. I will keep looking, Hank, but you and Chet can leave if you want to."

Jericho heard another voice in the house reply, "Sam, no one's leaving until we find that money. We all believe those Colbert boys probably hid that robbery money somewhere around here."

Jericho approached the partly open door, peeking around the corner of the doorjamb. But from that position, he couldn't see enough of the room, so he moved to the window and carefully raised his head, peering above the windowsill. The dirty glass panes distorted the images, making it almost impossible for him to make out anyone. However, he could make out the outlines of three people moving about the cabin's interior.

Tiptoeing back to the partly open door, Jericho reared his foot back and kicked at it with enough force to knock the door off its leather hinges. The door collapsed into the room's interior with a loud bang. Inside the room, three startled men froze mid-stride, all in shock when the door crashed. The scene lasted briefly before the three men galvanized into action and began snaking their hands down to their holstered guns.

In a blur of motion, Jericho's gun was in his hand and pointed toward the three interlopers.

"Don't move a muscle." Jericho yelled and proclaimed, "Don't even think about trying something foolish; don't make me have to kill any of you."

Jericho continued into the room's interior and demanded, "Who are you people, and what the hell's your reason for breaking up everything in this house? I know you're not the owners, and who permitted you to be in a cabin that doesn't belong to you?"

Nobody said a word for a few seconds, and then Jack entered from the rear of the house and fired two shots into the ceiling so rapidly that it sounded like one long shot.

Everyone ducked, even Jericho.

"My partner asked you all a question: The next bullets won't be in the ceiling. Start talking!" Demanded Jack.

The first man to speak was a long-faced man with a very high forehead. He said, "I'm Sam Darrin, and that man over there, pointing to a small balding man who was noticeably shaking, is Hank Bosman. The other man by the fireplace, pointing to a large, flabby man, is Chet Moore."

Sam Darrin glared at Jericho and became more vocal now that the initial surprise was over. He seemed to take charge of the situation, became the spokesperson for the three, and asked a question with as much bravado as he could muster: "We know who we are! I want to know, who in the hell do you think you are pointing guns at us?" Sam Darrin continued, not waiting for a reply from Jericho or Jack, "My friends and I have business here. You have no call to hold us or threaten us. We're law-abiding merchants from the town, and those Colbert boys owed all of us money for goods and services. We came to see if we could find any money to help pay their debts!"

"Fellows, this is just not your lucky day," Jericho replied. "The man behind you holding the gun on you is Jack Harden. Texas Ranger, Jack Harden, that is. And my name is Jericho Starr, Federal Judge Starr. As I see it, you're breaking the Law by trespassing on private property! And you've all just committed a criminal act and are under arrest!"

Jack instructed them, saying, "All three of you can slowly reach across with your left hand and fingertips, take those guns out of their holsters, and drop them on the floor in front of you."

Jericho spoke up, adding, "I would suggest that you heed his words, fellers. The Ranger doesn't kid around when it comes to arresting somebody, and please don't try anything stupid. The Ranger won't hesitate to lessen your time on this earth."

For a moment, the three men seemed to be evaluating just those options, but in the end, they took the most intelligent and least painful route. Each man, in turn, took his weapon from its holster, and one by one, they dropped the guns on the floor in front of them as directed.

"Step back away from those guns and lower your hands!" barked Jericho. And Jack, would you mind kicking their guns away from them just to remove any temptation that might get them killed."

Thirty minutes later, all three men had been tied hand and foot to the three beds in the room. One of the merchants, Sam Darrin, had begun hollering so much that Jack was forced to stuff an old sock he found into his mouth to shut him up.

Jericho and Jack sat at the table, watching the would-be criminals as they waited for Sheriff Johnson. A while later, the quiet was disturbed when someone outside fired two shots.

CHAPTER FOURTEEN

"Hello in the house!" a loud voice yelled.

Jack ran to the door expecting more trouble but breathed a sigh of relief; Duane had arrived astride a big coal-black Arabian horse. Jack waved for him to come on in.

After summarizing what had happened, the sheriff left with his three new prisoners, bound securely for transportation.

Jericho privately told the sheriff what the three men's jail sentences should be. "Two weeks of hard labor and a fifty-dollar fine for each. I expect this sentence will go a long way to making them all realize the error of their ways."

After the sheriff and his prisoners had left, Jericho started pacing and moving around the spacious cabin's interior. He stopped at various places within the room, looking under and around the furniture left standing; Jericho kept looking and poking around but never saying a word. Finally, he walked over to the table where Jack was sitting, bent over, and looked under it, saying, "I think I may know where them Colbert boys might have hidden the money."

He grabbed Jack's arm and began pulling him toward the back door.

Jack reluctantly followed, saying, "Where in the hell are you taking me, boss?"

"Just trust me for now," Jericho said, and soon the two men were in front of the dilapidated barn and corral. Jericho left Jack standing just inside the door, and he began looking around. He continued to walk through the dark interior of the barn. Jericho went up the ladder to the loft, and Jack could hear him walking around over his head. A few minutes later, Jericho descended the ladder and stopped before a large pile of hay, probably put there for the Colbert horses.

Jericho grabbed a nearby pitchfork and started probing through the pile of hay. He poked into the front of the mound, then went around to the back of the pile and began examining the back side of the hay mound.

Both men heard the audible clunk from the probing pitchfork. Jack thought the pitchfork might have struck stones on the floor, but he watched as Jericho bent down and began pushing the hay away by hand.

Jericho smiled and motioned for Jack to join him. When Jack looked over Jericho's shoulder, he exclaimed, "What the hell?"

Once the hay had been removed, four canvas bags, painted with the letters "US Army" on the side of each bag, were there in all their glory.

Jack was amazed, saying, "How did you know those bags were here?"

Jericho answered, "I just followed the obvious trail them boys left when they brought the bags into the house. I figured they first put the stolen bags on the table to count the money, and I saw the marks and scratches the coins had made in the wood. As I looked around the cabin, I noticed that under the table were many tracks made of muddy boots from all the rain we'd been having. The mud was mixed with pieces of hay, and I could see the trail of their boot marks as they led out the backdoor, which I assumed went to the barn."

"When I grabbed you to come with me, I had a hunch, and once I saw the trail of muddy bootprints that led into and from the barn, my hunch was confirmed."

Jericho stopped momentarily and continued, "There were so many tracks it took me a while to sort out their thinking, but the barn had to be the hiding place for the money. I found the loft was empty, and there was nothing up there but dust. When I came down, I noticed the muddy trail stopped in front of the pile of hay. I suspected the bags of money might be under the hay."

Jericho looked at Jack as he smiled, stating, "I got the impression that those boys were not all that smart or ambitious; I figured that the hay mound would be the most likely place to hide something without much effort."

"Jack, check the corral out back. See if the Colberts left any horses?" I feel pretty sure this is all the money they stole. A while later, Jack returned with a horse in tow.

Jericho stated, "That horse will come in handy when we return this money to Fort Justice. The horse can carry some of the silver and gold coin bags. I suspect that when the gang loaded the bags, each rider had to carry one bag to help distribute the weight. We should duplicate the weight distribution used by the Colberts. Each of us will carry one bag of coins, the spare horse we'll use as a packhorse to carry our gear and the other two bags of coins. We want to look like two riders with a packhorse."

Jack set about loading the packhorse and added several household items that he found: a large cooking pot, two frying pans, and a large dishpan. From the outward appearance, they would be just two men going somewhere on an extended road trip.

Jericho suggested, and Jack agreed that they would wait a while to see if any other citizens from the town might come looking for the location of the stolen payroll. They decided to wait until nightfall to begin their trip to Fort Justice.

Each man took turns watching for trouble while the other rested. Jack volunteered for the first watch while Jericho was catnapped.

Try as he might, Jericho couldn't sleep. His mind raced with plans and scenarios that might happen should anybody else show up to challenge them for the payroll.

A little while later, Jack approached Jericho's bed and announced that it was his turn to nap. Seconds later, Jericho heard some god-awful snores from the big man.

The two men waited the whole afternoon, but no one came. Each man was alert for trouble, but there had been nothing as the sun set low in the west. Just before the sun dipped below the skyline, it offered a beautiful burnt orange and pale-yellow vista.

Jericho told Jack, "I've been thinking about our situation and changed my mind. Let us take this money to the Bank in Dallas for safekeeping rather than the Fort. The bank's a lot closer, and the Dallas Bank and the Army can work out the details for the return of the money to Fort Justice later."

Jericho announced, "It's time we got started. Jack, would you bring the horses up to the front of the ranch house? I'll watch while you're busy, and we'll leave as soon as you're ready."

The two men were greeted by a moonless night and a dark clouded sky as their backdrop for the beginning of their long journey ahead.

Jericho knew traveling in darkness would become treacherous for the horses due to the terrain they would cross. As the pitch-black night engulfed them like a dark cloak, there were times during the journey when the blackness hid the riders from each other. Jericho used a rope tether as their primary safety line, keeping them from separating.

With Jericho leading the way, Jack soon discovered that the man in front of the procession had excellent night vision. Jack imagined that Jericho's vision could be compared to an Owl's and has no trouble navigating their way as the road ahead disappears into nothingness.

Jericho chose routes far from the main roads, guiding them around the off-road hazards. He also used densely wooded areas, navigating through tall grass and loose chaparral without incident.

The unceasing noise of crickets, frogs, and other night creatures became their early warning system at night, as did the endless horizons during the day. These methods allowed the two men to see any possible threats. Jack, bringing up the rear, always checked over his shoulders at their back trail, suspecting trouble, which thankfully never presented itself.

After five days of hard riding, five long days of Jack's complaints of his sore butt, and the lack of proper sleep, the early dawn of the sixth day found them amid grazing cattle, probably on someone's open range.

Jericho found a clean, small stream with several large trees in a semicircle that would give them a nice place to hole up. Jack walked around the campsite, inspecting it for pitfalls, and concluded that Jericho had chosen well. It was an excellent place to view their back trail and the trail ahead.

Later that afternoon, as Jack awoke from his nap, he grumbled, "Partner, I have a suggestion. Let's try to find softer quarters for our stay tonight. Walking those horses through that rocky terrain has made my feet so sore I can hardly walk. Sleeping on this hard ground has bruises on almost every part of my body. I need a good rest tonight in a soft mound of hay or a good bed."

Jericho smiled at Jack, thinking that Jack had probably slept in much worse conditions than any of these places, but he needed something to complain about and wouldn't mind something softer for the night himself.

Jericho agreed, saying, "There should be a few ranches further north along this way. We'll stop and ask if we can rest in a barn or stable for the night. We could get lucky. Someone may offer a hot meal, and besides, our horses will need hay and a place to rest without their loads."

CHAPTER FIFTEEN

Several more hours of travel brought Jericho and Jack to a spacious ranch house, which included a corral of horses attached to the barn. Other structures were also included to maintain a productive presence on a Texas prairie.

As the two men approached the ranch, they noticed a tall man standing in the house's doorway, holding a double-barrel shotgun. Jericho could also see a woman and two youngsters peeking out from behind the man with the gun.

"Hello in the house," called Jericho as the two men rode closer to the front porch. They were rudely greeted by the blast of the shotgun being fired into the air.

"Hold up there!" yelled the man with the shotgun. "We don't want any trouble from you all. I'll shoot you both if I must. We have nothing you could want, so be on your way."

"Mister, we don't mean you any harm," Jericho hurriedly exclaimed.

"My name is Jericho Starr, and this man with me is my partner, Jack Harden. We've been riding these horses for quite a while, and our horses need feed and water. If you're willing, we can pay for some home-cooked food. We also need to rest our bodies and horses for the night."

Jericho didn't want to elaborate, hoping questions wouldn't arise about why they had traveled all night and most of that day. Thankfully, the subject didn't come up.

The man lowered his weapon and invited them inside. Most Texas families settling out in the middle of nowhere would be happy to have company and someone other than themselves to talk to. Once inside, the head of the household introduced himself: "I'm Ian McQuinn, and this is my family." He pointed to each person as he introduced them: his wife, Linda, and their two kids, Mary and John.

Jericho assumed the McQuinn family seemed like any typical Texas family, willing to offer him and Jack the hospitality Texans were known for.

Ian, Jack, and Jericho talked on the porch while Linda McQuinn busied herself in the kitchen. Later that evening, toward sundown, they all sat down for a good old-fashioned meal consisting of fried chicken, black-eyed peas, mashed potatoes, and white gravy.

Jack was pleased; everything was to his liking, and the meal was delicious.

Jericho was happy to talk and listen to someone other than Jack for a change. Captain Harmon hadn't mentioned that Jack tended to jabber about almost anything.

Jericho liked his partner, but the family's conversations were a nice respite from their travels together.

Once the meal was over, Linda asked Jericho about his first name.

"The name Jericho is not a name you hear often. Is that your Christian name?"

"Yes, Mrs. McQuinn, it is, and there's a family story that goes along with how I got my name," ventured Jericho. "When I was born, my parents couldn't agree on a name for the first few days after my birth.

"My dad wanted to call me Jeremiah because it started with the letter J. My older brother's name is James, and my sister's name is Jesse, but my mother insisted that all the children's names were to be biblical.

"My mom wanted to call me John after the Apostle. Since both names would start with the letter **J** and, most importantly, would also be biblical, they were still at an impasse during those first few days after my birth.

"However, there was this one night when I was making a loud racket as most babies do; Dad told my mother he'd never heard such a racket in all his life. He told her jokingly that with lungs like mine, I could have brought down the walls of Jericho all by myself. They both laughed and carried on about the joke my dad had made. It was then and there they decided Jericho would be the proper and apt name for me, and that's how they settled on the name Jericho."

Jack and the whole McQuinn family laughed. They all enjoyed Jericho's story.

Jericho had to smile at them but began thinking and looking at his partner. He asked, "Since we're all talking about names, I'd like to know just how you came by Cactus Jack. You never shared that little detail with me yet."

Jack got a painful look on his face and began, "I was christened John Jefferson Harden; my middle name was in honor of Jefferson Davis of the Confederate Army. My dad got to calling me Jack when I was little, and the name stuck. The nickname was OK by me then, but when I was about sixteen, my two older brothers and I were helping our dad with the family business. We were busting wild horses to supply Fort Hood with all the horses we could find.

"There was this one horse that none of us could break, but being sixteen and rather stupid for my age, I proclaimed to all that I would break that horse or die trying.

"My father and brothers all laughed and called me crazy, but when my father left to deliver three dozen horses to Fort Hood, he left my older brother in charge.

"My brother saw the determined look on my face and told me to forget about riding that ornery backbreaker. "We've got a lot more horses to break. I can't afford to lose you as a hand while Dad's away."

A little grin appeared while Jack continued his story. "Once my father and the herd were out of sight, nothing my brother said could dissuade me from taking on that horse. I had become obsessed with making that horse tame. I headed for our corral on the run and got the saddle on that ornery critter, but the fool horse took over when I climbed aboard. I set my spurs into her flank. She hopped straight up, began crow-hopping for a while, and then suddenly lit out on a dead run.

"That horse was running full bore, straight for a bunch of cacti, and all I could do was hang on. That ornery horse had me right where she wanted me. The horse planted her front hooves and suddenly stopped, but I sure didn't. I hit those cacti on the fly and landed on my back onto what must have been the biggest cactus in the whole state of Texas.

"When I finally limped out of that prickly cactus patch, I pulled thorns out of my rear end as I looked for help to get the spines out. Unfortunately, my help was all rolling around on the ground, holding their sides, laughing like crazy. From then on, I was always known as Cactus Jack to my father and brothers, and everyone around the area picked up the name, and it stuck."

After the story, Linda, the wife of the McQuinn family, began shaking her head, trying with all her might not to laugh. That only lasted a second before the two kids began laughing with unabated glee, which produced peals of laughter from everyone else. Linda started to clear the dishes and told the men to retire outside to stay out of the way.

Ian took this respite to break out some homemade whiskey. As the three men sipped the excellent whiskey, Jack asked Ian, "Why the greeting with the shotgun? Do you always greet riders with that thing?"

"Sorry about that," replied Ian. "We're having many problems with my neighbor, Homer Adkins. Mr. Adkins has a big spread south of here. I've been told that he and his brother own it together, but the brother doesn't live around here, and no one has ever seen him." Ian continued, "Mr. Adkins is not much of a rancher, and I believe he wouldn't have a penny without his brother."

Ian paused briefly before continuing, "But his story took a different tone. Let me illustrate what I mean."

"Homer had an unfortunate accident. Since then, he's become bitter. His greed brought on the man's situation, and now he's alienated everyone in this valley."

Ian paused again to gather his thoughts and then began defining the problem as he saw it: "I believe Adkins' problems started when he built a dam to withhold the creek's water from the rest of us. He did this without asking our permission or before we could bring the courts to rule on our rights.

A while back, we had several tremendous rainstorms, one right after the other. The rains caused his dam to break, flooding most of Homer's ranch. To make matters worse, the dumb, greedy bastard had fenced in all the land below the dam. He had most of his livestock penned in right where the waters from the dam flooded the lower valley. His cows had nowhere to escape."

Ian shook his head, thinking about the senseless slaughter as he looked out at the last rays of the day's sun. He added, "Sometimes the good Lord looks down on us mere mortals. He must have seen the man's greed and decided to punish Mr. Adkins for his sinful ways."

Ian continued his horrific story. He talked about the things that had happened since the dam burst two months ago. Homer had started his rampage against anyone who owned property near him. At first, he tried to bully people off their land, but when that didn't work, he stepped up the pressure by killing livestock and having some of his men burn barns and corrals.

"He had two of my homesteading neighbors north of here killed. His men have no mercy. They killed these men in front of their families. Thank God they didn't kill the women, but they gave the women orders to pack up their kids with their belongings and leave. If they didn't, they were told the next time the men came, they'd finish killing all of them."

Ian said, "News travels fast around here, and now several other neighbors have abandoned their small homesteads. Just last night, another raid occurred at Sam Conklin's place. Adkins's men killed everyone, including the women and kids, and burned his farmhouse and barn to the ground! These raids are becoming more frequent, and now Homer and his gang have begun a full-out campaign to kill the homesteaders who don't abide by his warnings."

CHAPTER SIXTEEN

Linda McQuinn came out on the porch with cookies and a tray of hot coffee. She had overheard Ian's words but had her own opinion. "Homer's a ruthless man who doesn't think twice about killing anyone who gets in his way, and I hope we can defend ourselves when the time comes."

Smiling at his wife, Ian tried to assure her, saying, "Please don't worry, honey. My brothers and the rest of our clan have agreed to protect what is ours. We've armed ourselves properly and are in the first stages of setting up roving patrols to stave off Adkins' attacks."

"What are you and the others going to do about water for your herds?" asked Jack.

For the first time, Ian smiled and began telling another part of the saga. "We got lucky. My brothers and I dug wells to find our own water supply. Our first attempt didn't pan out like we wanted, but things changed dramatically when we dug a second well. We hit it big, and it was a gusher. There's enough water for everyone around here. We'll never have to rely on the stream Adkins tried to control for our water needs."

"The trouble is," Ian went on, "somehow Adkins found out about our new water source, and we're afraid he'll find a way to grab it and force the rest of us out."

Jericho, who had been thinking about the story the entire time, entered the conversation and asked, "You mentioned your neighbors and your clansmen. How many men can you count on?"

Ian's face lit up as he said, "When we came to this valley, my three brothers, my two uncles, six shirt-tail cousins, and their families all settled here hoping to raise sheep. But we soon learned that this is cattle country. Sheep and steers might get along to some degree, but people who raise sheep and cattle don't mix well. So, we reluctantly became cattlemen. Our families and neighbors now raise cattle for a living."

"All of my family have put down solid roots here, and we've all vowed to fight side by side, if necessary, to hold onto our spreads."

"Have any of Adkins' men bothered you yet?" Jack asked.

Ian thought momentarily and answered, "I think he had our fences cut and ran off some of my steers the other day, but I don't have any proof. And now things have gotten worse for Adkins," Ian continued. "We discovered the other day that Homer has a severe disease problem with the remaining steers from the dam breaking. His cows have some sickness, and none of us want his cows to infect our herds."

Jericho, who had been listening, absorbed all the information, bent close to Jack's ear, and whispered, "Looks like we dropped into another big mess here. We'll have to help calm this situation before we can leave."

Ian had left the porch for a moment to relieve himself. When he returned, he turned his rocking chair slightly, facing Jack and Jericho. He continued his story, explaining, "I left out some important details about the first well we dug. We didn't find water; it was more like a tar substance—black and slick. Later, I was told it was something called oil. What a mess that was. In the few minutes after we had dug the hole, we were up to our asses and covered with that black, gooey stuff before we knew what was happening."

Ian's eyes brightened as he added, "A neighbor from back East knew something about the sticky tar stuff, telling us that this black stuff is now worth some money. I contacted someone who knows about this oil, and he came from Dallas to evaluate our findings. The company has offered me a lot of money to let them develop the oil. And now, there might be another problem for me. I think Adkins knows about the oil, and that's another reason why he's so all fired up about running me off my land."

A worried look came across Ian's face as he thought about someone like Homer, who would do anything to increase his wealth.

The conversation waned, and finally, Jack and Jericho conceded to their host how tired they were and thanked him and his family for their hospitality. Refusing beds in the ranch house, Jericho and Jack were satisfied with bunking in the barn.

Later, they entered the barn, stripped the horses, stowed their saddles, and began pitching enough hay to feed them properly. They used another pile of hay to hide the money bags and set their saddles and gear atop the straw as an added safeguard.

Jericho didn't want to have to explain what the bags contained, and he sure didn't want anybody to mistake him for someone who might have robbed a bank.

Their work was completed, and Jack and Jericho mounded up plenty of hay for two soft beds. The hay would be a welcome respite from the hard ground of the previous day.

Early the following day, Jack awoke first and went out to the side of the barn to relieve himself. He then noticed two riders approaching from the west. As the riders neared, one of the men began calling out, "Hello in the house! Mr. McQuinn, please don't shoot. We need to talk. Please hear us out."

Jack saw the ranch's door open, and Ian McQuinn emerged carrying his double-barrel shotgun. Ian yelled, "Leave now. I don't want any trouble. Get off my land. I'm not about to let your boss run me off. I'm here to stay."

The two men put their hands over their heads and begged Ian to listen. "Mr. McQuinn, wait a minute and hear us out. You've got us all wrong. My name is Gerry Vargas, and this here is Tad Kindel," he said, pointing to the rider beside him. "We don't have much time. Please listen to what we say. Mr. Adkins and six of his gunmen are about to come over that hill yonder.

We overheard them talking last night about how they would get rid of you and your family come morning, but we left early this morning to warn you."

"Mr. McQuinn, we're just ranch hands, not killers!"

"How far behind you do you think those riders are?" Ian asked.

"Not more than fifteen minutes," replied the man called Vargas. "Mr. McQuinn, we want to help, but we're just ordinary ranch hands. Don't be offended; we don't want to be here when the killers come your way."

"Thanks for warning us when you did. You boys had better get along now," Ian replied.

Jericho roused himself, saw that Jack was gone, heard the commotion outside, and joined Jack at the fence. Assessing the situation, Jericho told Jack to stay there and watch his back. He ducked through the fence and came behind the two men, nervously glancing toward the west.

"Boys, I overheard what you said to Mr. McQuinn. Would you be willing to do Mr. McQuinn a big favor when you leave?" asked Jericho. "Would you ride to Mr. McQuinn's brother's ranch on your way out and tell them they must get here as soon as possible?"

"Sure thing, mister," replied the cowboy named Tad Kindel. "I know where Mr. McQuinn's brother lives; you can count on us to deliver your message."

The two riders turned their horses and urged them into a dead run, heading northeast toward McQuinn's brother's ranch.

About that time, Jack eased himself through the rails of the corral fence and hurried over to where Jericho was intently talking to Ian McQuinn. Jericho explained what everyone had to do as he took charge of the situation and gave orders to Ian and Jack.

"It looks like McQuinn's got some big trouble headed this way. We don't have much time before Homer Adkins and his six hired guns arrive, and I believe they're out for blood. Jack, Captain Harmon bragged that you're good with that Henry rifle, and I think this would be a good time for us to find out just how good you are."

Jack smiled at the challenge from Jericho. He was ready for anything and said, "Have no fear, partner. I'm the best shot with a rifle in all of Texas. So, what do you have in mind?"

Jericho laid out his plan, instructing Jack, "I want you to go into the barn loft. That will be a good spot with a good view of the front of the house. From that perch, you'll have a bird's-eye view of any riders that get this far onto the property. Your job is to cover us from that loft while Ian and I try to get behind them. I don't want you to kill anybody unless we must. I want you to wing the first rider; that should stop the rest of the gang long enough for us to get into position."

Turning to Ian, he said, "Ian, you should send your family out of harm's way. When Homer and his hired killers get here, it's going to be chaos, and you don't want to worry about your wife and kids while trying to protect your property at the same time. To be safe, send them to your brother's place."

Jericho knew it would be up to the three of them now. They would have to defend the Ian ranch until Ian's brothers arrived.

Quickly, Ian had his wife and both kids by his side, kissing and hugging them—maybe for the last time. Soon, his family was safely aboard three good horses, headed for his brother's ranch. It didn't take long for the three men to get ready. Jack was already in the barn's loft, and soon after, Jericho and Ian were able to carry out Jericho's plan.

Ian had retrieved his shotgun and a handgun and gathered as many shells as he could carry; the rest he stuffed in his pockets.

Jericho looked at the scattergun, knowing nothing was better than a shotgun to instill fear. At close range, his shotgun would do much damage to many people.

Jericho waved until he got Jack's attention and pointed to a stand of trees about 500 yards west of the barn. With Ian in tow, Jericho raced for the trees that he thought would provide good cover—a big surprise he hoped they could spring once Atkins, and his men arrived.

Once the two men were hidden in the trees, he laid out his plan for when Atkins and his killers passed by.

Jericho had given Jack risky instructions—to wound, not kill. He knew it was a gamble, and things could turn ugly instantly.

Jericho told Ian, "When Jack fires from his perch, that will be our signal to come out from the trees and present ourselves. We should be behind the gang. Jack can cover us should anyone get brave enough to challenge us while we're in the open."

"Are you ready, Ian?" asked Jericho.

"Yes, sir, I'm ready to make my stand," Ian replied, his determination clear.

CHAPTER SEVENTEEN

Five or six minutes later, seven men on horseback passed the trees where Ian and Jericho stood in hiding.

As the gang of seven approached the house, a shot rang out, and one of the riders in front collapsed forward on his horse with a bullet hole in his shoulder. The shot had the desired effect on the rest of the riders. They all came to a hurried halt and began looking around for the shooter. Disoriented by the fear of additional fire from the unknown source, they were just about to scramble off their horses when Jericho and Ian quickly positioned themselves directly behind them.

Jericho's threatening voice proclaimed, "Stay on your horses and don't move. Any sudden move or attempt to reach for your guns will get you killed. Keep your eyes looking straight ahead."

Jericho continued, "No one has been killed yet, but that could change in a heartbeat if you don't do what we say."

One of the men began to turn in the saddle, and another shot rang out. The rider lost his hat due to that wrong move and poor judgment. The hatless man grabbed for the top of his head, gasped, and was relieved to find there was no blood.

The men astride their horses realized—and had the good sense to know—that they were in deep trouble, trouble so close that they were looking at a no-win scenario.

"Homer Adkins, turn around!" Jericho yelled as he addressed the seven men. He hoped the right man would turn when he addressed the gang.

Slowly, one of the riders began to turn. He was quite a bit older than the rest. The older man glared at the two men who had so blatantly braced them.

Jericho focused on the older man and said, "I suspect you're the leader of this gang of thugs. I want you to tell your men to do exactly as I say, or you will be the first man I kill."

"Please do as he says," was the shaky reply from the older man.

Jericho ordered the others, "All of you can turn around now. Slowly put your hands above your heads. I want to see both of your hands empty."

All the other men on horseback raised their hands in unison. Turning, they could see the two men with guns in hand, pointed straightaway in their direction.

Ian stood guard with his shotgun pointed squarely at the riders, and Jericho covered Adkins with his pistol. It didn't take a genius to see they were well covered.

"I know, Ian, but who the hell are you, mister? And what business do you have meddling in my affairs?" demanded Adkins. "I don't have a quarrel with you, whoever you are," the man continued with his blustery reply. "I'm Homer Adkins. I made Mr. McQuinn a fair and generous offer for his land, and I'm here to make sure he takes what was offered. My cattle need the water Ian and his brothers found; they can't live without it."

"Damn you, Adkins, it's not yours to have or take!" replied Ian.

Jericho couldn't wait any longer. The situation and their advantage might not last much longer. He challenged Adkins, "Homer, throw your weapon away and dismount." Adkins hesitated momentarily, but thinking better of it, he threw his sidearm to the ground and dismounted.

Jericho knew the battle was half over and instructed the rest of the gang to slowly lift their guns from their holsters with the tips of their fingers. Then, they were to throw the weapons on the ground in front of the horses. "Do it now!" barked Jericho.

Each man complied with the commands one at a time until all the weapons were in the dirt. Jericho waved his gun at the hatless gunman, saying, "Starting with you, get down, and the rest of you follow one at a time."

Each man, in turn, dismounted, trying as best they could to keep their hands raised. They struggled with the chore of dismounting with their arms above their heads. It was quite a feat, but they sure didn't want to give the two men with all the guns a reason for a bloodbath.

The wounded man was helped from his saddle by two of the other riders, but they immediately put their hands back up for fear someone might start shooting.

"What do you suggest we do with these fellers?" Ian asked Jericho. "They did come here to threaten me and maybe even harm my family; what's going to happen next?"

"Let's start with them in a position where they can't be of harm," Jericho said. All you men get on the ground face down and stay in that position until you're told differently. Jack came running up to join the group, saying, "Hello, boys." Jack told the man lying on the ground, "Now there are three of us to cover your mangy good-for-nothing hides."

The hatless outlaw turned his head around and looked up at Jack. "Was that you who shot my hat off?" "Where did you take that shot from, anyway?"

"Why from that barn yonder, the barn's loft to be exact," remarked Jack. "Why do you care?"

"Mister, that barn is five hundred yards if it's afoot."

"How did you manage to take my hat off without blowing my brains out?" the hatless outlaw said. "That's an amazing shot from that distance."

Jack smiled and winked at Jericho, saying to the man on the ground, "How do you know I wasn't trying to shoot your horse and just missed?"

The hatless man gulped and blanched several shades of white as he closed his eyes and upchucked whatever he had for breakfast that morning.

Jack took over guarding the prisoners with the shotgun.

Jericho and Ian stepped back a bit to talk. "What do you think we should do with Adkins? " Ian asked.

Jericho looked off into the distance, searching for Ian's brothers.

"The first thing we'll do is you and Jack can help me tie these owl-hoots up. And when your brothers get here, they can help watch them until Jack and I can get the Law out here."

"Your ranch isn't that far from Dallas, and it should only take us about half a day to get to the sheriff's office," commented Jericho. "I know the sheriff there, and he's a good man. He won't hesitate to get out here when I'm finished telling him what Adkins was about to do. He has plenty of room for Adkins and his gang in jail."

"And I'm sure that Adkins and the rest of his gang will be sent to prison for their past deeds. Just as soon as I can arrange things with the Circuit Judge assigned to Dallas/Fort Worth, all the things you told me about him and his men—killings and driving folks from their lands—I believe there might be several candidates for the gallows."

"Once Jack and I tell the Judge in Dallas what Mr. Adkins was involved with around here, his fate is sealed. He's probably going to have a death date with the hangman."

A little while later, Ian's brothers appeared over the horizon, and within a few minutes, they were on-site and ready for action.

Ian introduced his brothers to Jack and Jericho. He heaped glowing praise on his two guests, telling them how thankful he was for their invaluable help in keeping his family and himself safe from being killed and his place destroyed.

After several handshakes and back slaps, Jericho and Jack begged off further Clansmen business and left Ian and his brothers to guard the prisoners.

"We need to get going to have as much daylight as possible," remarked Jericho. And with Jack at his side, Jericho returned to the barn.

Once the two men were inside, they quickly saddled their horses and prepared the pack horse for travel. Together, they strained to load the money onto the pack horse, hefting those bags, which wore out both men.

Jack finished camouflaging by hanging the big dishpan and pots again, and Jericho checked the doorway to see if everything was in order. Once he had completed his check, Jericho and Jack mounted and returned to where Ian's brothers stood guard.

"We'll be back as soon as possible with the sheriff," promised Jericho.

The two men set a quick pace, and the sun's golden-yellow ball began its long descent into the western sky.

Later, as the sun had dipped below the horizon and darkness was close at hand, Jericho and Jack rode into the city limits of Dallas. Their first stop that night would be the sheriff's office. They rode to the middle of town until they reached the building with the sign that read Jeremiah Pitts, Sheriff, Dallas, Texas.

"I think I know that old law dog!"

"If that's him, he's been here a long time," Jack remarked. "Come to think of it, I believe he's been here ever since I joined the Rangers."

They entered the door to the office and were greeted warmly by Sheriff Jeremiah Pitts, who began laughing and loudly proclaimed, "As I live and breathe, is that you, Cactus Jack? What brings you this far from the Ranger post in Lufkin?"

CHAPTER EIGHTEEN

Smiling at the laughing man, Jack proclaimed, "Jeremiah, this is my new partner, Jericho Starr. Federal Judge Starr, to be exact."

"Hell, Jack, no need to introduce Jericho; I've known him long before I ever met you," replied the sheriff.

The sheriff grabbed Jack's hand and slapped him on the back. Jack was startled, and a look of disbelief crossed his brow. It was a bit of a shock that Jericho was so well known.

Jack proclaimed, "Jeremiah, you used to be the fastest man with a gun I had ever seen until I met Jericho Starr. He's better than the both of us put together. Jericho is now the fastest man with a gun, the likes of which I've ever known."

Jack continued, laughing and adding, tongue in cheek, "Jericho, did you know that Sheriff Pitts was so wild and ornery? The Founding Fathers of Dallas were so scared of Jeremiah and his gun that they didn't know what to do with him, so they convinced him to become sheriff."

Sheriff Pitts looked at Jack and winked, saying, "Thanks for that wonderful assessment of me. And, of course, there's a lot more to that story he's not telling you, Jericho."

The sheriff changed the subject, asking, "Did Jack call you Judge Starr? When did this happen? The last time we bumped into one another, you were still in the Army, and I thought I knew just about everything that goes on around here. I know all the judges and lawyers in these parts. I don't recall hearing about you or anything about a Federal Judge being assigned to this area!"

"I just got assigned; it's not been made official by all the authorities yet," Jericho replied. "My new territory will cover most of the northern part of Texas and the border states." Jericho pointed at Jack and said, "Jack has agreed to be my chief deputy, and he will soon become a Federal Marshal. We're going to Fort Justice, where Jack will be sworn in as a new Federal Marshal."

Jericho asked, "And I believe you know Chief Justice George Bidwell? He's in charge of putting together a group of judges and marshals to enforce and uphold the state's laws. Our assignment is to help the other lawmen and rangers in the state bring an end to some of the lawless elements operating in Texas."

"Hallelujah!" cried Jeremiah. "I've been waiting a long time for people in this state to get off their lazy ass and take some positive action."

"Now that I think on it, Justice Bidwell stopped here last month; he said he was forming some Justice Force. So, you two guys. Where's the rest of your men? Are they coming later?" asked the sheriff.

Jericho had to smile at that question and replied, "Not right now, maybe, but soon." Jericho thought momentarily before answering, finally saying, "For now, we're it. Then there might be enough marshals and judges in Texas to end most criminals abiding in our state."

Jericho changed the subject as he related the goings-on at McQuinn's Ranch and told the sheriff what must be done as quickly as possible.

The sheriff agreed, saying, "Tomorrow morning, my deputy and I will go out to his ranch. We'll bring those assholes back here for a trial. If you're willing, I could use your help. Would you be willing to come along tomorrow?"

"Hell yes, you couldn't keep us away!" remarked Jack, and Jericho smiled and agreed.

Jericho remarked, "Sheriff, now that that's settled, where could I expect to find an honest banker in this town?"

"You'd be looking for a person named Henry Jamison," replied the sheriff. "It is about seven o'clock now, and he's probably over at Marge's Diner. What do you want from a banker?"

Jericho replied, "I have some urgent business that needs to be completed at the bank as soon as possible."

Jericho and Jack left the sheriff's office, promising to meet there the next day and be ready to go at first light.

After retrieving their horses, the two men walked to the diner and secured their mounts at the rail in front of the eatery. When they entered and were greeted with the pleasant aroma of freshly cooked food, both men realized how hungry they had become from the day's events and the long ride to Dallas.

Jericho spotted the man Jeremiah had described. He was the only man in a suit, and as they approached him, Jericho asked, "Are you Henry Jamison, the banker?"

"Why, yes, I am," the man replied. Then he looked up to see the two strangers standing at the edge of his table.

"Why do you ask? What's so important that it can't wait for tomorrow?" demanded the banker. "If you have business with the bank, it's too late. We're closed right now. I will have it open promptly at nine o'clock tomorrow."

The banker's attitude irked Jericho as he glared at the rude man.

The banker turned around in his seat, focused on his meal, and without looking up, told the two men, "Kindly leave me alone. My meal is getting cold." He stabbed a piece of steak and forked it into his mouth. This was the banker's way of dismissing the two dusty men.

Jericho pressed the conversation, saying, "We have something that needs to be secured in your bank tonight. I need you to open your safe right now!"

"What is this? Is this some holdup?" The startled banker blanched and said, "You men have picked the wrong bank. I won't be bullied into opening the bank or the vault. You might as well look for another bank in town to pull your heist on."

"Mr. Jamison, my name is Jericho Starr, Judge Starr, and the man beside me is Jack Harden." But something Jericho said caused the banker to frown. His brow wrinkled, and he thought deeply as he tried to remember what Jericho had said.

The banker was brought to attention when Jericho proclaimed, "We are duly authorized officers of the State of Texas. I'm a federal judge, and Jack here is my deputy. I'm ordering you to get your butt up from that chair and take yourself over to your bank. NOW!"

Jericho wouldn't let the banker off the hook, saying, "I don't have time to mess with you. We haven't eaten all day and are both hungry and tired."

Turning to Jack, Jericho asked, "I think it would be a good idea to have Sheriff Pitts join us at the bank."

Jack left the eatery and hurried to get the sheriff. Jack thought about what Jericho had said as he approached the sheriff's office. *It made sense that the sheriff should be there to witness what would happen shortly. The sheriff would be the perfect person to vouch for both of them.*

Reluctantly, the banker pushed his meal away, got up slowly, and followed Jericho into the street. Jericho untied the horses, grabbed their reins, and led them while following the banker down the street. They soon stood in front of a building with a sign-out front marked with big letters: Dallas Bank. The banker, along with Jericho, started to enter the main door. That's when Jack and the sheriff arrived, and all three men watched the banker unlock the main door.

The three men followed him into the bank's main lobby. Once inside, Sheriff Pitts stopped the banker and began explaining the presence of Jack and Jericho. He first vouched for the two strangers and then told the banker that Jericho was a new judge and had the authority to demand that the bank vault be opened.

That information satisfied Banker Jamison, who lit several hurricane lanterns around the bank's interior. He took one lantern with him to light the gloomy interior and motioned for the men to follow him into the room with the vault.

Jericho took Jack and the sheriff outside while the banker lit several other hurricane lamps inside the vault room.

Jericho asked the sheriff, "Would you mind helping Jack and me carry the bags we have stored on our horses? I'll explain the load contents when they are securely in the bank's vault."

Jack carried two bags while the other two men struggled to bring one in. It was a long way from the street to the vault, but once the bags were unloaded and safely stored in the vault, the sheriff figured out their contents when he looked at their markings. Then he asked, "Where did you get all that Army money?"

Jericho began, "It's a very long story, but the gist is that it was the payroll for Fort Justice. It was taken about a month ago by the Colbert Gang, and Jack and I caught up with them in the town of Crocket. Jack recognized some of the gang members, but I can safely say that when he tried to arrest them."

"Sheriff Pitts, you won't ever have to worry about the Colbert Gang anymore. Those stupid men in the gang challenged Jack, and he took care of the situation. Now, there aren't any Colbert men left to deal with."

Jericho added, "We've been traveling with these money bags ever since, and that's why I wanted to keep this money safe and secure rather than have these bags tied to our horses."

"There won't be a problem with my bank," ventured the banker. "The bank's vault is the best and safest anywhere! I got myself a Linus Yale cast iron vault, and it's got one of those new combination locking devices," continued the banker. "It's one of only two in the state of Texas! The men who brought my vault and installed it claimed there was another vault, and I believe it was shipped to a Chester Adkins in Emerald City."

The banker brightened as he recalled the question that had bothered him in the eatery. He hadn't remembered asking, "Excuse me, Mr. Starr. Is Starr your family name? By chance, are you related to the Joshua Starr family? Does the Starr family own that big spread northwest of here—the one that's so big it extends over into Oklahoma? That ranch is supposed to be the biggest cattle ranch in the western half of Texas."

Jericho frowned at the banker and reluctantly commented, "That spread you're discussing is only partly mine. My brother and sister work the ranch full-time, but I haven't been much help since I joined the Army. I would appreciate it if you all would keep that information to yourself."

Jericho took Sheriff Pitts outside and explained, "Now that we've taken care of this business with the bank, and once that situation out at the McQuinn ranch is taken care of, Jack and I will be headed for Fort Justice."

Jack, however, was puzzled as he looked at Jericho, his boss. He wondered, just who the hell was this guy? Jericho sounded like a rich man, a very wealthy man indeed. Jack asked himself what the hell Jericho was doing in the U.S. Army. Now that his boss was a federal judge, it gave him plenty to think about.

CHAPTER NINETEEN

Jack was interrupted from his deep thoughts when he heard Jericho tell the banker, "Good, all is settled! I'd be obliged if you would provide me with a receipt for this transaction for the Fort's records." When he had the receipt in hand, Jericho felt like a large stone had been lifted off his back. The money was safe, and they could devote the rest of their time in Dallas to clearing up that situation at McQuinn's Ranch.

Leaving the bank, Jericho and Jack both thought about how hungry they were. Making their way back to the diner, Jack looked around and noticed the lateness of the night had cleared out most of the patrons, and plenty of tables were open. The two men sat briefly, reading the diner's specials, and both decided on the pot roast with mashed potatoes, new white corn, biscuits, and gravy.

After they had ordered and the hot meal was delivered, Jack smiled across the table at Jericho. "Partner, since you're so rich, much richer than I'll ever be, you have the pleasure of paying for my meal tonight and maybe from now on."

Jack's thoughts wandered throughout the meal, but he kept his feelings bottled up and didn't discuss Jericho's wealth anymore.

Later, as they entered the local hotel, Jericho secured two rooms and paid for them without Jack asking for his money. Standing next to the doors to their respective rooms, Jack looked at Jericho and said, "Partner, you've got much explaining to do. I want to know a hell of a lot more about you than I know now."

Jack had one question he couldn't wait to ask: "Answer me this one thing now: Why in the hell are you taking on all these dangerous jobs when you have more money than God?"

Jericho wasn't surprised by Jack's statement and didn't want to put him off. There would be a better time for this discussion. Still, he knew he had to say something, or Jack would burst at the seams. Jericho responded, "Jack, sometimes men need to fulfill their inner desires. I have always wanted to give more than I ever received, and serving in the Army helped feed that call from within. It has always been a lifelong desire of mine to be a judge. I have much to contribute, and I strongly believe I can make a difference."

Jericho began to grin, saying, "Let's not worry about my wealth right now. I'll tell you everything you want to know once we finish the McQuinn situation."

However, Jack went to bed with more questions than answers.

Jack spent much of that night tossing and turning, unable to sleep. When he finally did sleep, he had dark and mysterious dreams that belied the bond between him and Jericho.

The next day, well before sunrise, Jericho knocked on Jack's hotel room door. "Hey in there, are you ready? Remember, we've got a date with the sheriff this morning."

Jack wanted to yell back for Jericho to go away, but he thought better of it and began getting dressed. A few minutes later, he opened the door to an empty hallway. Where had Jericho gone without him?

Jack suspected that Jericho might be one who seemed never to sleep, but he was always full of energy, no matter what time, place, or situation. Leaving the hotel, Jack headed for the sheriff's office, mumbling, "It's pitch black out, and it must be about five in the morning; what in hell's so pressing that a man has to be up this early anyhow?"

Jack continued walking toward the sheriff's office. He mused to himself, "Why am I bitching and fussing so much?" This was about the time of day he was usually up at the Ranger Station; however, Jack did feel the effects of the previous night's restlessness. He felt the irritability of a troubled man, and he still struggled with his present disposition. Jack suspected that his feelings were very apparent. Indeed, his feelings would show on his face, and how he carried himself would be noticeable.

"Morning, Jack," came the good-natured greeting from Jericho as Jack entered the sheriff's office. "Sorry about last night."

Seeing the dark mood written across Jack's face, Jericho asked, "Are you all right, Jack? You look mad enough to haul off and bust something. I suppose what happened last night upset you, and you still have a lot on your mind, but I promise you, Jack, I will come clean about everything tomorrow night."

Jack considered what Jericho said. He pushed his feelings aside, knowing the answers would come soon.

Jericho and Jack were introduced to Tom Jenkins, the sheriff's deputy, who would be traveling with them to the McQuinn ranch.

And just as the sun began to peek above the horizon and the dawn of a new day began, the four men left the sheriff's office and mounted their horses, heading for the McQuinn ranch.

Jack's mood remained somber. Although he usually carried the brunt of the conversation, he remained sullen and mute.

The sheriff tried to jolt Jack into a conversation, saying, "Jack, do you remember when we first met?" The sheriff continued, "You had just begun as a Ranger and were like a giant fish out of water."

Jack retorted, "If you don't mind, Pitts, I'm not in the mood for much talking, and I don't feel all that well. I didn't get much sleep last night." Those words confirmed to everyone that Jack had a lot on his mind.

Sheriff Pitts and Jericho knew neither man should press the issue further, so Jack wasn't included in their conversations for the rest of the trip.

Once the four arrived at the McQuinn Ranch, Sheriff Pitts and his deputy, Jenkins, introduced themselves to Ian and his

Clansmen. A lengthy conversation centered around the events leading up to the problems that Adkins had caused Ian and his family.

Ian related the terrible problems that had caused deaths and destruction of the other ranches around the McQuinn Clan's properties.

The sheriff and his deputy gathered the prisoners, and Jack and Jericho said their goodbyes to the McQuinn Clan. Jericho wished them all good luck in the future. The four men, with their prisoners in tow, headed for the path westward to return to the sheriff's offices in Dallas.

They traveled without incident, and later, after depositing the prisoners into waiting cells, the deputy took the wounded man over to the doctor's office for treatment of the bullet wound in his shoulder.

Jericho's time was then taken up signing the appropriate affidavits. He was sure to include the charges of the murder of the two neighbors and the attempted murder of Ian's family, and he finished his summary with suspected arson and the theft of cattle.

The sheriff placed Jericho's sworn statements and recommendations in his file drawer.

They all agreed that Ian's problems with Adkins should be a thing of the past; Homer and his men would probably be tried for murder. If they were found guilty, they would all be hung as soon as the courts of Dallas set the date and time.

Jericho thanked the sheriff and the deputy for all their help that day.

Jericho and Jack mounted and rode out of Dallas to begin the long ride northward to Fort Justice. Jericho thought to himself that it was going to be a long ride if he didn't change Jack's mood. He anticipated that the long trip would take five and a half days.

Jack was quiet during the first day's ride, and Jericho didn't push the issue.

But as they rode along, he composed what he would tell Jack when they camped that evening.

The sunset that night was spectacular, and even Jack's spirits seemed to lighten with the vista before them. Once again, Jericho found a good camping spot. The site had all the amenities a good scout would look for: water, plenty of game, trees for shelter, and a defendable front should they run across hostiles.

It was Jericho's turn to cook, and Jack's task was to hunt for their supper.

Jericho had just finished getting a good fire going when he heard a shot a short way from the camp. A few minutes later, Jack emerged from the woods with a giant wild turkey slung over his shoulder.

Each man set about preparing their evening meal. Jack cleaned the turkey for roasting and dug up wild onions and greens. Soon, everything was ready, and both men sat quietly while finishing the meal, which had been delicious.

Later, as the fire burned to glowing embers and became a breathing, pulsing yellow light, the two men settled beside the still-warm fire to drink some freshly brewed coffee.

Jack chose this time to speak: "Well, partner, you promised yesterday to come clean about just who and what you're doing in this wilderness. You could and should be living the high life. I can't wait any longer. Tell me, why on earth would a man as rich as you want to roam around Texas, living like someone who's more like a saddle bum or a poor cowhand?"

"Settle in, Jack; this will be a long story," replied Jericho.

CHAPTER TWENTY

Jericho began telling Jack about his grandfather and his family. It took several minutes for him to give a brief history of his grandfather's journey from Philadelphia to Texas. Jericho explained that his grandfather had vast knowledge of the American Plains Indians.

Someone from the Bureau of Indian Affairs who knew of my grandfather's knowledge contacted him and asked him to become an Indian Agent for the Comanche Tribe in Oklahoma and Texas.

He couldn't believe his good fortune and took the job, promising to send for his wife and son once he was established with the tribe. His travels took him to Fort Worth, Texas, where he was introduced to an expert guide named Two Bears.

Several days later, they were able to locate the Comanche Tribe. Once near their camp, Two Bears entered and spoke to the tribe's chief on my grandfather's behalf. In the following days, my grandfather earned the trust of the tribe's chief and was allowed to stay and live among the Comanche.

My grandfather convinced the Chief of the Comanche Tribe to make changes that would impact their lifestyle. He began by substituting beef cattle for the decreasing buffalo. He then showed the Comanche how to manage their herds for their future needs, knowing that this would eventually be the mainstay for the Comanche people. They went from nomadic people to landowners with large herds of cattle to sustain them.

My grandfather also convinced Government officials to allow the Tribe to have the new Winchester 66 model rifle for their protection. The other tribes still tried to steal what the Comanche owned, but with the latest guns and roving patrols, the warriors learned tactics to repel these attacks upon the Tribe.

"Whoa, hold on, partner, "I need to use the woods for a minute," ventured Jack as he ambled close to the tree-lined creek. As Jack left the campfire, he said, "When are you going to get to the part about you being rich?"

When Jack returned, he looked at the blazing fire and quipped, "You weren't kidding when you said this was a long story. You got enough logs on that fire to last all night."

Jericho resumed his story.

My grandfather was made an honorary member of the Comanche Tribe, and he then sent for my grandmother and their boy, my father.

The Tribe gave them a homestead close to the Comanche Nation and supplied Indian workers to help with their ranch.

However, soon after they had settled, there was a severe outbreak of Measles, and my grandmother died along with many of the Comanche people. All that remained of the Starr family was my grandfather Samuel and his son Joshua, my father.

Jericho went on to explain how important his grandfather was to the Comanche. When my grandfather died, the Comanche Nation wept for him as one of their own.

My father, who was about twenty-two, married a missionary woman, and they had three children. My brother James was their first child, and my sister Jesse was the second. However, my birth mother died giving birth to me. My father was devastated, and soon, out of necessity, he asked the new Chief of the Comanche, Running Wolf, for goat's milk for my food. The Chief did something even better: He offered his daughter, White Fawn, to look after me.

White Fawn had recently lost her husband, who had been killed in an accident. She had just given birth to a baby girl named Little Doe, and White Fawn and Little Doe came to live with us permanently.

My dad and White Fawn fell in love, and she became my stepmother. She still lives with us at the ranch, and Little Doe, my half-sister, is now a part of my family.

Jack said, "That's all well and good, but when will you tell me about all your money?"

Jericho cut his family's history short and tried to get the information Jack wanted, saying things changed rapidly. There was a huge demand for beef for the next 60 years, and our joint cattle endeavors quickly multiplied. Between the Tribe and our ranch, we controlled most of the cattle in the State.

Jericho thought he should also explain to Jack what he had gone through growing up to finish the story of how he became a judge.

When I turned thirteen, my grandfather, Running Wolf, asked my father if I could come and live with the Comanche; my grandfather would become my mentor and teacher. Age thirteen was the time of the Comanche trial into manhood. I joined my grandfather at the Comanche camp and began to undergo the trials required of all males at that age. I was much larger than most Comanche teens and had more speed, agility, and quickness than the other males of the Comanche.

Running Wolf was a tremendous warrior and a great leader of his Tribe, but he was also a loving and wonderful friend to me. I soon outdistanced the rest of the braves, and with his help and guidance, I became his star pupil. Through his teachings, I became the best hunter and the best all-around tracker of the Tribe.

My grandfather was incredibly proud of my accomplishments, and when I was sixteen, the Tribe honored me by giving me the title Buffalo Star.

When I was seventeen, I returned to live with my parents because my father had become ill. My brother needed help running the ranch while my father was mending. His sickness lasted several months, and luckily my father recovered.

My father was on good terms with the Commander of the Regiment in Fort Worth. He asked the Commander for a recommendation for my appointment to attend a Military

School called West Point Academy. I was ready and excited to begin my assignment. It was something new, and I couldn't wait for the challenge.

After graduation, my first post with the Army was at Fort Hood, Texas, where I became the commander of an Artillery Company that was sent to support the North in the Civil War. My next position was as an advisor to the Indian Affairs Department.

I was then reassigned as a Provost Marshall for the Eastern Texas area of Houston, where I was stationed. It was there that Judge Bidwell contacted me, and you already know the rest.

Jack wiped his brow like he had gone through some ordeal, saying, "Whew, that's one hell of a story, but you haven't answered this question. What the hell are you doing out here in this wilderness? You have all that money, and instead of basking in the good life, you're out here risking life and limb trying to bring justice to this wild god-forsaken country."

Jericho ended Jack's speculation by saying, "Riches and wealth are not something that I earned or even wanted, but they allow me to help others in need and practice what I love, the Rule of Law.

Jericho went to relieve himself. When he returned, Jack was fast asleep, smiling down at the big man, sure he had picked the best man for the job ahead.

Looking out into the darkness, his thoughts focused on the next day's journey, where they would finally meet with Judge Bidwell.

CHAPTER TWENTY-ONE

Jack beat Jericho awake the next day and thought this event was amusing. He knew Jericho's penchant for always being ready before everyone else. Jack had his horse saddled and his bedroll tied on just as Jericho passed by to relieve himself.

Jack couldn't let it be, try as he might. He couldn't keep himself from a slight grin and said, "I thought you were going to sleep until noon the way you sawed logs this morning."

"It won't ever happen again," Jericho said nonchalantly over his shoulder. "It's your fault, after all, that I couldn't get my usual sleep. If you had your way, I would never get any sleep having to satisfy your need to know everything about my life or the lives of my family."

Both men were in the saddle and headed northwest just before the pre-dawn gloom began to lighten the skies with their pinkish-amber streaks. Sunrise would usher in the beginning of a new day.

After days of riding, they reached the stumps of trees around Fort Justice. The trees had been cleared for several hundred yards in all directions. These same trees were the cut logs used to build the Fort walls, the barracks, and several other buildings to house animals and store goods and weapons. Numerous log bridges spanned several small creeks on the road to the encampment. With the trees cut down, the defenders of the Fort could see anyone approaching from a long way off in all directions.

As they approached the heavy double doors of the gates, Jericho paused and called out, "Hello in the Fort."

A lone soldier leaned over the edge of the log wall. He recognized Jericho at once. Coming to attention, he saluted and called out for the guards below to open the gates. A few minutes later, the two men rode into the middle of the compound, and two soldiers came running to secure their mounts.

Jericho and Jack dismounted, and Jericho asked the soldiers to take their mounts to the blacksmith and have him check them over for stones or burrs in their hooves.

As the soldiers left with their horses, the two dusty men headed for the office.

Jericho led the way as both men walked up the stairs to the porch and entered the door marked *Headquarters Office*. Jericho approached the orderly behind the desk and informed him that Judge Bidwell was expecting them.

The orderly slid his chair back. Getting up, he went through another door at the back of the room and returned quickly, saying, "The Judge is waiting for you. Please follow me!"

Jack's first impression of Judge Bidwell was puzzling. He had expected a much older man, but the Judge appeared to be only ten or twelve years older than himself.

"Welcome back, Jericho," the man behind the desk said. "Jericho, tell me what happened to Captain Harmon. Harmon didn't say much to me in his wires; he only wrote that he was sending one of his best instead of himself."

"It's a long story, sir. Why don't we all sit down? I'll explain what happened when I was searching for a deputy. By chance, did Captain Harmon's wires explain anything about Jack?" Jericho asked.

Jericho assumed that the wire messages had explained little about what had happened and even less about Jack.

Standing straight, Jericho correctly introduced Jack and explained what had happened to his friend Harmon.

Judge Bidwell interrupted Jericho's report and asked if they wanted refreshments. They both nodded.

The Judge called for the orderly to bring some cool water, and Jericho continued his report. He began answering several more questions from the Judge. Jericho concluded with information about the stolen payroll and its secure whereabouts in Dallas.

"Wonderful news!" replied the judge as Jericho finished.

The judge turned his attention to Jack. "Mr. Harden, all I have are these wires from Captain Harmon recommending you, and he told me that you are one of his best Rangers."

Looking over at Jericho, the judge asked, "Judge Starr, what do you want to say about Mr. Harden?"

Jericho began his assessment of Jack, saying, "Jack has already proven to me that he is going to be a great asset, and he's going to be a great addition as a new marshal. Jack saved my bacon the other day during a shootout in Crocket with the Colbert Gang. His quick thinking kept me from getting killed. He's the right man for the job."

Judge Bidwell rose and proclaimed, "Based on your glowing assessments, Mr. Harden, I have all I need to confirm your appointments."

The judge called the orderly in, telling him to fetch several documents Jack must sign.

Twenty minutes later, Jack became a brand-new Federal Marshal for the State of Texas. The judge also confirmed his blessing of Jack as chief deputy assigned to Jericho.

Shaking hands with Jack, the judge clapped him on the back and ushered them outside so he could smoke.

He told the orderly to bring him the bottle of Scotch from his desk drawer and three glasses. The orderly set the bottle on the table and filled the glasses with the brown liquid that Jericho was now quite fond of. Raising his glass, the judge toasted the two men, saying, "To your health, gentlemen. May your association always be in the interest of justice and most beneficial to the State of Texas!"

Jack thought as they stood on the porch: *I rode all this way, thinking there would be a more extensive and formal ceremony. Becoming a Federal Marshal only takes a few words, a slap on the back, and a few papers to sign. The whole thing took only a few minutes, and the deed was done.*

But Jack thought the Scotch was excellent.

Jericho and Jack were shown to their quarters. Jack, being Jack, told Jericho he was ready for a little nap. Jericho, however, had more to discuss with Judge Bidwell and said he would see the big man later for supper.

Jericho returned to Judge Bidwell's offices. His boss looked up from his papers and said, "Jericho, I was just about to send for you. I have more information about Emerald City. But what you told me about the situation is most troubling. Based on what I know and this new information, Chester Atkins is immersed in various criminal activities.

"It's quite a coincidence that I sent an investigator to look into some things I heard about Chester Atkins several weeks ago. Later, I sent two deputies to help find this man, but I haven't heard from anyone. This situation happened well before I asked you to become a judge. The judge continued, "Many more things were coming to light."

"I was told something significant happened at that Comanche encampment up by the Oklahoma border. And I think you know of that camp. Didn't you used to live there? Are you still a member of that Comanche tribe? I was told that Atkins and his gang of thugs may have raided the encampment and killed several braves.

The judge said, "Chester Atkins seems to have a hand in everything bad that's happening. There are other reports of several homesteaders missing, stagecoaches and Wells Fargo depots being robbed, and settlements raided for their livestock. Atkins's name keeps coming up every time."

"However, Jericho, "Judge Bidwell remarked with concern, "It's this business with the Comanche Tribe that worries me. I can't afford for the Indians to stop the production and distribution of their beef. That would leave a huge hole in our meat supply. Too many people rely on their cattle for food."

Bidwell continued, "Jericho, as soon as you and Jack are ready, I want you both to visit the Comanche encampment. I need a firsthand assessment of what's happening there."

Jericho was about to leave when the Judge spoke. "Come to think of it, this will be your first assignment together," he said, smiling. "I don't have to tell you how dangerous this assignment will be. Be careful, and don't get yourselves killed before you two get started."

When Jericho returned to their quarters, he found Jack fast asleep. He left quietly, not wanting to wake the giant. He had other priorities: he needed to visit the stables, to make sure their horses would be ready for the journey to Emerald City.

Jericho's next stop was the quartermaster's office for supplies. His last stop was a trip back to the Judge's office. He had forgotten something essential and hurried there. He realized he had inadvertently omitted information from his report.

Jericho sat facing the Judge, saying, "Judge, I forgot to tell you about a situation that arose when we were in the Dallas area. I told you before about how we intervened in a squabble between Mr. McQuinn and another man involved in that fracas. His name was Homer Adkins. What intrigued me the most was the discovery of oil on McQuinn's property."

Jericho continued, "I've had time to think about that oil discovery. I'm inclined to wonder what kind of impact this might have on the surrounding homesteads and ranches in that area."

Judge Bidwell looked at Jericho with an all-knowing smile. Standing up, he explained, "I have had other reports about oil being discovered in and around Dallas/Fort Worth. Mark my words, Jericho, this oil discovery will bring prosperity—and major headaches—to our state! I'm sure that I will have to appoint a lot more marshals to keep law-abiding citizens protected from the greedy land grabbers and cutthroats that will surely infiltrate our fair state."

Jericho left the office and headed for the stables to load the supplies. He talked with the blacksmith, who assured him the horses were fine for travel. An hour later, he returned to the barracks to wake Jack. But when he entered, Jack was awake, pacing the floor with a troubled look.

"What's bothering you?" asked Jericho.

"I've been thinking about how the two of us could get into Emerald City without that gang of owl-hoots knowing," Jack replied. "If they were to find out you're a Judge and I'm a Marshal, it would turn into something akin to suicide. Not to mention, it might get a little tricky keeping the lead flying our way before we even have a chance to judge the situation."

"Jack, I have been thinking the same thing ever since I learned about Emerald City and the malicious and deadly Homer Adkins."

Jericho and Jack sat around the table, reviewing their packed supplies. Jack felt that everything Jericho had packed would be adequate.

However, during their mission assessment, they agreed that getting into the town might be relatively easy. Still, the minute they started asking questions or poking around in the town's business, someone would surely become suspicious.

CHAPTER TWENTY-TWO

The two men rode through the gates of Fort Justice just after reveille. Their travel would take them northward, east of the Emerald City limits.

Jericho had traveled there before. He estimated the ride would take about seven days. They would have to follow the well-used roadway route for stages and most commerce in the northwest. On the sixth day, Jericho judged they were approaching their destination. Jericho stopped at the crossroads, where one road led to Emerald City, and the other led to Clarendon.

Jericho explained to Jack that the junction was close to their objective. Jack gigged his horse forward before Jericho yelled, "Stop, Jack. Emerald City is not that far ahead. I don't want to alert anyone who might be connected to Adkins. Let's find a good spot to camp for the night, somewhere that we can watch the road."

Jericho shook his head and gigged his horse to draw abreast of Jack, saying, "Where were you going?

Jack stopped short. "Dammit, I guess I've been riding too long. Sorry, boss, it's been a long several days, and my mind was on whisky and women. I'm just groggy and tired."

Jericho passed on a response and returned his attention to finding a good camp. He knew this part of Texas very well. He had ridden these hills looking for strays and later rode with the Comanche tribe to hunt.

Several miles later, Jericho found the spot he sought, a small clearing next to a creek with plenty of shade trees. This was a good place for the horses to blow and munch the grass that grew abundantly along the creek's shelf.

"I've been here before," Jericho told Jack. "When I was learning the ways of the Comanche braves, my fellow braves and I camped and fished this very stream. This spot will be far enough away from Emerald City not to alert anyone there, and we can see anyone traveling on the road. It will allow us to ride to the town without much trouble for the horses."

As they rested, the two men began formulating a workable plan for getting into the town. Several discarded plans later, Jericho called a halt to their plan-making.

Jack took the respite to sack out under an oversized elm. Jericho was about to join him when he saw something west of their position, traveling the road to Emerald City. He retrieved his binoculars for a closer look.

His scowl and worried brow quickly turned into a big smile as the object he had spotted became six colorful wagons he had seen before.

He slapped the hat covering Jack's face and told him, "We got company." Pointing at the wagons approaching, he said to Jack, "Those are some wagons the circus show uses. I think it's the same circus show where I met Amanda. That's the gal I told you about while we rode to Crocket City."

Little swirling tufts and curling dust followed the caravan as the wagons neared. The dust settled when the wagons reached the knee-deep grass. Eventually, the wagons slowed, finally stopping just off the road near the two men standing.

"Hello in the camp," yelled the man driving the lead wagon. "Can we water our teams here?"

Jericho waved back, yelling, "Yes, yes, step down and rest awhile. There's plenty of water in the creek. The ground is firm here, and the horses won't have trouble getting to the creek's edge."

"Hi again," came a female voice.

Both Jericho and Jack looked past the first wagon to the second wagon. Jack looked pleased, and a familiar smile crossed his face—the unique smile he always had for pretty women.

Amanda was quite a beauty. Always a gallant gentleman, Jack was about to help her down from the driver's seat. That's when Jericho broke Jack's bubble of ardor and desire.

Jericho began waving and smiling. He told Jack, "That's the gal I was telling you about. She's the one who told me about Brad Colbert's whereabouts when I visited the circus."

Jack regained his wits and said to his partner, "You told me she was good-looking. But, boss, you didn't bother to tell me how gorgeous she was." Shaking his head and grinning at something he thought funny, he directed his comment to Jericho, saying, "You know, ole buddy, you seem to attract all the gorgeous women. I frankly can't see what those gals see in you.

From a guy's perspective, I think you're kind of." Jack waited for Jericho to look in his direction before saying, "Prissy."

Jack couldn't hide his smile or the twinkle in his eyes after speaking. But truth be told, he thought Jericho was one of the most stately and handsome men he had ever met. For that very reason, he couldn't help busting Jericho's chops about this gal.

"Jericho, who's the tall, dark, and handsome drink of water standing next to you, darling?" said the gal he had first met as she approached where they were standing.

Putting a hand on Jack's shoulder, Jericho proclaimed, "This here is Cactus Jack Harden, the partner I told you I was going to the town of Lufkin to find. But if a gal were smart, she'd run for the hills. Ole Jack here tends to break the hearts of all the females." Jericho laughed.

"You should talk," jeered Jack.

"Madam, let me properly introduce myself. My Christian name is John Jefferson Harden, but I prefer Jack. The business about 'Cactus' is something my brothers called me, and it's their joke. If you like, we can spend some time together, and I can tell you why it's stuck with me all these years."

Jericho just shook his head. Knowing Jack as well as he did, he grabbed Amanda's arm and began walking away as they exchanged pleasantries.

Jack stood for a few moments, looking forlorn. But another gorgeous woman appeared from the back of one of the wagons. Within a minute, she was standing next to Jack, rubbing her eyes from sleep — beautiful blue eyes, to be exact.

"Who are you?" exclaimed the blue-eyed gal, smiling sweetly.

Jericho and Amanda had returned, and before Jack could speak, Amanda said, "This is Norma Jane Albright. She's one of the star attractions of our show." She smiled at Jack, who was making himself noticed. She interjected, "Norma dances the seven veils for our adult guests. Jack, I can tell you this: she's been known to raise the temperature in one of our tents twenty degrees doing her dance."

"Norma Jane, this is Jericho Starr," Amanda said, pointing at Jericho. "He's the guy I told you I met in Marabee Junction."

Norma Jane moved quickly near Jack, grabbed his arm tightly, and proclaimed, "This one's all mine, Amanda. You got

Jericho. And you know I like my men very tall—I mean, real tall—and he's handsome to boot."

Norma Jane had to crank her neck to look up at Jack. She batted her eyes, then put her hands on either side of Jack's head, brought his head down to her level, and kissed him on the cheek, saying, "Honey, there's a lot more where that came from; just wait and see."

Jericho looked at their surroundings and suggested that they move into the shade. Even though it was close to sunset, the heat in the open was fierce.

The four of them, arm in arm, began walking toward the cluster of trees near the creek. Amanda suggested that they would be more comfortable with some blankets. Jack, being the ever-suave rascal he was, volunteered for the errand.

Amanda pointed at the second wagon, telling Jack that the blankets were stored in her oversized trunk near the middle of the wagon.

Jack returned soon with an armful of blankets. Jericho helped him spread the blankets, and they all sat down and continued their conversation in relative comfort. The discussions ranged from how well the Circus was doing to what Jericho had been doing and what Jack would do as a new Marshal.

Jericho looked at Amanda with curious eyes and asked, "Amanda, are you still performing your act as a trick shot artist for the show?"

Amanda reluctantly answered, "Not right now. I've taken over running the show since my dad's on the road setting up the towns for the show. My dad and I are partners. We own the Circus, lock, stock, and barrel together. I had to give up the trick shooting from horseback several weeks ago, just after I met you."

Norma Jane broke into the conversation, saying, "Amanda can't be shooting at targets and riding a horse. She can't do much of anything strenuous right now. She injured her shooting hand lifting and pulling on all that heavy gear that was being loaded into the wagons a while back."

"Norma Jane, I asked you to keep that information to yourself," Amanda said with a scowl. "I haven't even told my dad yet, and I expect I'll have to break the news to him when he returns from Emerald City tonight or tomorrow." Looking over to Jericho, she continued, "My dad's the one who sets up all our dates for the show in advance, while I'm supposed to take care of the day-to-day operations."

Jericho changed the subject and asked, "How well do you know the people in Emerald City? And do you know a man named Chester Adkins?"

"Why, yes, we know of him. We've been playing Emerald City for several years," Amanda answered. "We return every year about this time; the townspeople love us. Last year, we had our best gate in Emerald City when we stayed two extra days at the townspeople's request. But now we must deal with their new Mayor, Chester Adkins."

Amanda's face showed disgust as she continued, "I try to stay away from that guy as much as possible. I get the impression that most people in the town have a morbid fear of the man."

And I didn't like how he looked at me when we first met. Adkins is a real creepy guy. He has a small army of mean-looking men working for him. I tell you the truth, they all give me the willies. He calls them Deputies, but I'm not fooled. They all look like thugs to me. And there's something funny going on in that town. Adkins is in the middle of everything. He's taken over running the town completely."

"The only good thing about that bad situation is we're good for business. I'm sure glad he likes us because I have this funny feeling that if Mr. Adkins didn't want you, there would be hell to pay at some point."

CHAPTER TWENTY-THREE

The four of them spent several hours talking that afternoon. Jericho learned some other information that might be helpful later on. They abruptly stopped talking when Jack noticed a lone horse and rider approaching. Jack was quick to see that the man had good taste in horses. He was riding a magnificent Palomino.

As the rider approached the encampment, he waved to all the men tending the livestock near the wagons. "Hello in the camp," yelled the man. When he came abreast of where Amanda was waving and smiling, he called out, "Amanda, I've been looking for you for over two hours. I expected you further down the road."

Amanda ran to where the man on horseback had started to dismount. He swung down from his saddle and turned just in time to catch the running girl in his arms. "Amanda, I'm glad you're all right. I was apprehensive when I couldn't find you at the place we agreed on."

"Father, we're in good hands. These nice men asked us to rest here a spell, and I think you remember Jericho?"

Looking at Jericho, the man said, "He does look familiar. Isn't that the soldier boy we met in Marabee Junction?"

"Yes, Daddy, he's the same one. We came upon their camp, and he and his partner asked us to join them. I was sure you could find us. But if you didn't show up in the next hour, I was going to send one of the drivers after you."

"Thank you, gentlemen, for keeping my daughter entertained and safe. Please let me introduce myself. I'm John Prentice, and you've already met my daughter Amanda." Looking over at Jack, the man said, "I know Jericho, but I don't believe I know you."

"I just met him today," Amanda said. "His name is Jack Harden, Daddy. He's a Federal Marshal, and he's been traveling with Jericho as his chief deputy."

"Well, Jack Harden, I mean Marshal Harden. Young man, just what should I call you?"

"Mr. Prentice, Jack will do fine," Jack replied.

"Harden, I've heard that name somewhere before," questioned Amanda's father with a frown. "Were you ever a Texas Ranger? I think I heard of someone by that name being the best with a rifle in all of Texas."

"That's me," piped Jack with a big smile. "At least somebody heard about me and appreciated my talents. Jericho here doesn't give me much credit."

Jericho had had enough. He sighed and proclaimed, "The man's got a big enough head now. I don't need anyone else to help feed his big ego."

Changing the conversation to something more urgent, Jericho said, "Partner, let's see if we can come up with supper for all these nice people." Jericho and Jack left the wagon party to scout the area for wild game for the supper meal. A few hours later, they returned with several pheasants, a small doe, and a wild hog.

"Whatever's your pleasure, we've got bird meat, hog meat, and venison," Jack stated. "Who's going to help us fix the meal?"

Smiling at Amanda, Jack said, "We just kill and skin them. Someone else can cook them. " He shucked his load of game to the ground.

Everything worked out well. It was the Jacobi family whose turn was to fix the meals that night, and they were excellent cooks. Everyone enjoyed the feast. Later, the people involved with the circus, the performers, and their two new guests sat around a roaring campfire.

Jericho was curious and asked who the main attractions were and what they did in the circus. The Jacobi family were jugglers; their act included two brothers, their wives, and their uncle and aunt. Then there were the Wilsons, a husband-and-wife knife-throwing act. There were the Sorensons, a whole family of wire walkers: a mother and father, two boys, and two girls. The Powell family had a horse act. Then, there was Norma Jane, the veil dancer. Of course, Amanda, the main attraction, was a trick-shot artist. Her father and several clowns doubled as drivers. And there were several more minor acts that rounded out the performers. Of course, there were also teamsters, band members, and roustabouts.

The conversation was lively, and it was evident that everyone in the troupe liked each other. There was plenty of laughter as each group talked about their homes and homelands. It was fascinating to hear how they had come to be with Amanda and her father's circus show.

John Prentice learned about his daughter's accident during their talk around the campfire. Jericho noticed how worried he was about Amanda and her act. Her act was a big part of his show, and now, he would have to call upon other performers to fill in for her missing act. Based on the conversations, Jericho knew that Amanda was one of the main attractions. The people in Emerald City would be expecting her to perform.

Jericho motioned to Jack to follow him, and the two left the campfire to a spot where no one could hear their conversation. Jericho told Jack that he had just thought of a way to get them into Emerald City unnoticed, saying, "If you were to take Amanda's place as the sharpshooter for the show, I think there wouldn't be much scrutiny from Adkins' men."

Jericho continued, "Besides, I need to visit the Comanche Nation anyway, and I could join the circus once you're established as part of the troupe."

Jack was in complete agreement. Armed with that idea, Jericho approached John Prentice and his daughter just before they were bedding down for the night to explain his plan. "Jack assures me of his abilities with his rifle and sidearm. I thought he could be a temporary replacement for Amanda." He felt obligated to confide in them and tell them their real reason for trying to get into Emerald City. "If you agree to my plan, we will try to get in and out without causing any problems that would be dangerous for you or your people."

John Prentice thought momentarily and then asked, "Since we know what you and your partner have planned, do I have your assurance that my people will be safe? But I could sure use Jack as a fill-in until Amanda's injuries heal."

John Prentice turned to his daughter and asked, "Amanda, don't you agree that this would be a big help in our situation since you're unable to perform your act?"

She jumped at the suggestion. She thought Jack would be an excellent replacement and assured her father that she would start teaching Jack her routine tomorrow. Amanda grabbed Jericho by the sleeve and pulled him away so her father wouldn't hear them talking.

"Where will you be tonight?" she asked Jericho.

Jericho replied, "When we talked the other day, you told me the circus would travel to Clarendon for a two-day engagement. Then, it would be another two days before you were due in Emerald City. Sometime during those four days, I plan to join you. I will be there before the show gets to Emerald City.

Amanda, when I return, I will blend in as one of the drivers or roustabouts for your show. I'll be leaving early tomorrow to visit his brother and sisters at their ranch. It's a long way, and getting there will take a while.

"Well, lover, that leaves us with tonight," Amanda said, batting her eyelids with a seductive smile. "Why don't you join me in my wagon right now? We shouldn't waste this opportunity. I've got a big bed in that wagon, and it's big enough for both of us. And as I recall, it's the same one you slept in before." Amanda chuckled to herself, saying, "We didn't do much sleeping when we first met." Amanda said, "I'm looking forward to having you all to myself tonight."

With a kiss on her cheek, Jericho exclaimed, "I cannot refuse a beautiful woman such as you. I was looking forward to your company tonight. I'll join you as soon as my horse is bedded down properly. And I need to speak with Jack about my plans for tomorrow."

Amanda smiled ear to ear, saying, "You can see to your horse, but talking to Jack will be next to impossible. He went with Mary Jane to her wagon just before you came to talk with me. And I bet he doesn't want to be disturbed by you or anybody else about now," Amanda said as she looked at Jericho with a wicked gleam.

Jericho laughed, saying, "You're right. I'll just be seeing our horses tonight, too. I wouldn't want to interrupt Jack's fun session with Mary Jane. He'd be impossible to live with if anyone messed with him tonight."

As the last light of the golden sun began to color the sky, it also became the muted light that showed through the wagon's canvas, outlining the two lovers as they kissed. The inside of the wagon was smoldering hot from the long day of blistering heated air. Added to this heat in the wagon, the two lovers' bodies made the inside of the wagon almost suffocating.

Jericho and Amanda quickly shed their clothes. Their two bodies were coated with sweat droplets.

Amanda reached out and grabbed Jericho's hard stalk and sank to her knees as she pulled his manhood into her mouth.

Jericho gasped, reached out, and grabbed one of the wooden ribs that held the canvas to steady himself. The fact that he was standing on bedclothes made him wary of falling as he held her head with the other hand.

Amanda pulled off his manhood and said, "Don't you dare relieve yourself in my mouth; you have other things you should do while you're hard." The wickedness in her voice brought his mind back from his dreamy pleasure to the demand from Amanda. Jericho lowered Amanda onto the bedclothes until she was flat on her back. Amanda opened her legs wide to give him access to her heated core, and kneeling before her, Jericho placed his hard root to the entrance between her legs and pushed himself as far into her as he could.

It was Amanda's turn to gasp as she stifled her moan by turning her head and burying her head into a nearby pillow. Neither Jericho nor Amanda wanted to alert anyone of their lovemaking, but they both knew that noiseless sex was almost impossible. Jericho began to withdraw his manhood to a position just inside her and then sink back into her molten inner being.

Over and over, he repeated this movement, ever faster and faster, as Amanda matched his thrusts for thrusts until she became so delighted with pleasure that she had to muffle her screams of delight into his shoulder. "Stop, stop! cried, Amanda. You have to pull it out now! This time of the month, I am very fertile; please don't come in me!"

Jericho barely heard her pleas in time but reluctantly withdrew his manhood as his essence squirted all over her belly and breasts. Amanda looked at the white trails of his seed and laughed as she dipped her fingers into the pool of his hot seed. She said, "That was close, my God, what a load you produced."

Jericho lay beside her and watched in fascination as she wiped her body with the bedclothes, saying, "I will surely have to do laundry tomorrow."

Amanda looked happy and fulfilled as Jericho took her into his arms and hugged her. Knowing he would soon have to get back to the business at hand, Jericho let himself relax, and Amanda soon became quiet. The two lovers rested until they were both asleep.

Jericho must have sensed the temperature change in the morning, as it had awakened him. He arose quietly, leaving the beautiful, sleeping woman who had shared her bed with him the previous night. His thoughts began to relive the experience and how their lovemaking had left him both exhausted and yet exhilarated.

The early morning ground fog greeted Jericho and his mount. It quickly consumed him and obscured the rider and the horse from anyone's view. As he rode, he looked forward to seeing his homestead and his family.

Jericho began to focus his attention on the landscape as he wove his way through the hills and fields along his path. It had been a long time since he had passed this way, and the ride brought back vivid memories of his time on the ranch, his stay with his grandfather, and his time as one of the Comanche. He smiled to himself as he rode toward the Starr ranch.

CHAPTER TWENTY-FOUR

The ride to the Starr ranch was uneventful. His view of the vista before him was spectacular. Jericho knew that for miles around him, in every direction, he was on Starr Ranch property. He saw several workers going about the business of a typical ranch day. As he rode further, many workers stopped to see the lone rider approaching. Then, in recognition, they began to wave and shout their greetings.

The big ranch house lay just ahead. Jericho hadn't been home for many years. He saw that his brother had stepped onto the porch a long way off. He looked around, trying to figure out what the yelling from the ranch hands was all about. When he saw who the rider was, surprise seized his features. He jumped off the porch and began running toward Jericho, yelling and crying simultaneously.

"Jericho, is that you?" his big brother's voice choked with emotion. "It's been so long!" he cried, brushing tears from his eyes with his shirt sleeves.

When Jericho dismounted, his brother grabbed him and lifted him off the ground in a big bear hug. They staggered in some dance until James broke the hug. Putting his hands on Jericho's shoulders, he happily said, "Let's hurry to the house. White Fawn, Jesse, and Little Doe will be glad to see you. This is such a wonderful surprise."

When Jericho was inside the ranch, the greetings from his sisters and stepmother were equally tearful. Jericho couldn't keep the tears back, even if he had wanted to. Eventually, things calmed down, and they all gathered around the table for a late afternoon lunch.

The talk centered around Jericho and what happened since his last visit. He told them everything he could remember. He ended by telling them about his new appointment as a judge. He smiled as he included the description of his new partner.

The conversation soon shifted to the real reason he was at the ranch.

Jericho began, "I was sent here to investigate the killings of the Comanche braves. I'm also here with Jack, looking into the rustling of cattle and the robberies in this area."

"You came to the right place," James remarked. "We've had our share of troubles lately, and it's not just the Comanche being attacked and robbed. We lost two hundred head of steers this month, by my count. I heard that the other spreads have had attacks also."

Jericho told his family that he had to leave the next day to visit Running Wolf. He hoped his grandfather could shed some light on the happenings of the Comanche Nation.

Changing the subject, Jericho asked his brother, "James, have you ever heard the name Chester Adkins?" Before James could answer, his sister Jesse spoke up and angrily proclaimed, "He's a devil and downright evil. He's been here a couple of times wanting to buy our ranch. Several of his so-called deputies were with him the last time he was here. We had the Indian workers escort them off the ranch at gunpoint. Adkins is not a man you can trust. I know he's responsible for driving a couple of our neighbors from their land this past year."

James was quick to add, "I agree with Jesse. I believe he's behind the rustling that's been going on, but we don't have proof. I have a gut feeling Mr. Adkins is something more than what he lets others see."

Jericho agreed and explained, "My boss, Judge Bidwell, has received several complaints about Adkins and his gang of deputies. He's convinced that Mr. Adkins is the source of all the trouble in this area."

Jericho suggested that James double the Indian workers patrolling the herds, but he asked his brother, "Don't do anything until I get a better handle on the situation."

Late that night, after a beautiful time with his immediate family, Jericho said his goodbyes to everyone. He would be leaving very early the following day.

Now that he had been assigned to this area of Texas, he promised them that he would visit more often.

While the darkness was turning gray just before dawn, White Fawn got up and joined him as he was saddling his horse in preparation to leave.

He was about to climb aboard when she grabbed his shoulder. She had to stand on her tiptoes to kiss him goodbye and whispered, "Please be safe. I have a bad feeling about this awful man, Chester Adkins. I had a dream about him this week. He came into my dream like the shadow of death. The darkness of this man exudes evil all around him."

"Remember this, my son: "You are a mighty warrior of the Comanche and a chosen warrior who has returned. Running Wolf, your grandfather, will expect you to take your rightful place at the Council. He has always valued your wisdom and knowledge."

Jericho left the ranch just as the sun peeked over the ridge he was riding.

His ride to the Comanche Nation would take him through the flatlands and across the Prairie Dog River. That vista would give way to rolling hills, which would change into the mountains' foothills that marked the Comanche Nation's entrance.

He followed a path he knew all too well. He passed between two prominent peaks that signaled the entrance to the Comanche homeland. As he continued to ride, he was met by three armed Comanche riders. They stopped him short with a rifle shot in the air.

There was a sudden awareness of one of the Indian riders. He recognized Jericho.

"Buffalo Star. It is I, Pony Who Walks. Do you remember when we took the trials of manhood together? It's a good omen that you have returned to the Comanche. Running Wolf will be pleased when he sees you."

Pony Who Walks ordered the other two riders to stay as guards. He told them he would accompany Jericho through the pass and into the Comanche camp. The two men rode abreast as they entered the camp's outskirts. They continued through the camp until they reached a large wooden structure: the Council's Lodge.

Jericho dismounted, but as he turned toward the lodge, he noticed an Indian and a white man tied securely to two large posts near the Council Lodge. From their looks, they had been there for quite some time.

Running Wolf, his aged grandfather, appeared from within the doorway of the Council's Lodge. He threw his arms into the air and proclaimed, "The Great Spirit has brought me my grandson. Buffalo Star has returned."

Jericho ran to his grandfather and hugged him. He lifted the old man off the ground and proclaimed, "It is good to see my grandfather; it makes me happy to be home. I have returned to the Comanche this day; it is an honor to see you, my chief."

Several warriors emerged from other tents and wooden homes around the camp. They joined the two men, proclaiming Jericho's arrival a good omen.

The Medicine Man, Two Crows, began waving the sacred Eagle Feathers into the campfire smoke. It was the Comanche invitation and a sign for the Great Spirit to bless the event of Buffalo Star's return.

Running Wolf began speaking to all those around him, proclaiming, "Let us prepare the way for a Council Meeting." Grabbing Jericho's arm, Running Wolf led him to where the circle of warriors would assemble, and motioned for him to sit at his side.

As they waited for the Council to form, Running Wolf looked at Jericho.

Running Wolf saw that Jericho was troubled and asked, "What troubles you, my grandson? Please tell me why your expression is so worried?"

"Grandfather, what has happened? Why did the Comanche have those men tied to the posts? Who is that white man?" he asked.

"The white one was captured when his gang of men sought to steal our cattle five days ago," Running Wolf answered. "He has confessed much since his stay at the pole in the hot sun. I have learned his name. He is called Curly Mosher, and he has told me he was part of the gang sent here by Chester Adkins. The other tied to the pole is Walks By Water, and I am sad to say he is of the Comanche. Walks by Water has betrayed his people. He was seen talking to Curly Mosher a day before the raid. He confessed that he told the rustlers how to get around our roving sentries. Curly and his gang stole seventy steers before we could run them off. When the raid was over, we found that the gang of thieves had killed three of our braves."

Jericho told his grandfather and the council about his new position as a judge. He explained what that would mean to everyone in his authority area, including the Comanche. He then told the council that Judge Bidwell had sent him to the Comanche to discover the truth about the rumors. What the judge feared had been confirmed.

CHAPTER TWENTY-FIVE

Running Wolf looked at the men tied to the post and spoke. "You can have the white man to do with him as you want. However, Walks By Water must endure the punishment of the laws of the Comanche Nation. He must die for his betrayal of his people and his role in the killing of our people."

"The Council was meeting today to determine how he should die. My son, it is wrong that Walks By Water should die and the white man should live. But this is a judgment of the White Man's Law. We will respect your decision on the matter."

Jericho replied, "Grandfather and council members, I have no time to take Curly Mosher to Fort Justice for a trial. I have the authority to render a judgment now," Jericho said. "Separate the white man from Walks by Water. I will have Curly Mosher hung for his crimes against the Comanche people. The Comanche can do with Walks By Water as they choose."

Running Wolf thought for a moment. He began speaking to the entire council. "I believe that a hanging judgment is a fitting punishment for the white man. And I believe hanging should also apply to Walks By Water. His hanging will put an end to his treachery. The Comanche believe there is no honorable afterlife for Walks By Water from a hanging death."

The whole council agreed to the punishment. Both men were dragged to a large tree away from the camp and unceremoniously hung. Afterward, Walks By Water's body was removed. It was taken far from the camp and left in the open to be eaten by vultures and other wild animals. This was yet another punishment for Walks By Water's spirit, which would wander forever.

Jericho had a quick thought. He had something in store for Curly Mosher's body. He had asked that the body be wrapped in a blanket soaked in a salt solution that would preserve the corpse for an extended time.

Running Wolf ordered the things that Jericho had requested. After wrapping the body and blanket, they placed it on a canvas tarp and draped it over a pack horse.

Jericho had explained to Running Wolf that keeping Curly's body might be useful when he finally arrived in Emerald City.

Running Wolf and Jericho retired to the Council Lodge to be alone, but during their conversation, Jericho asked more questions about the man named Adkins.

His grandfather's responses confirmed what he already knew: Adkins was the real cause of all the Comanches' troubles over the past year.

Jericho and Running Wolf put their heads together and devised a tentative plan of action that Jericho could use later. The plan involved using some of the armed Indian guards. Jericho asked that these braves be alert for his call to action. He would send word, either by himself or through someone else, with further instructions.

Jericho thanked Running Wolf for the pack horse that transported Curly's body and bade his grandfather and the rest of the Comanche farewell. He promised to return often after they had disposed of the problems with Adkins.

Jericho rode out of the hills with the pack horse in tow. He found a spot on a hill overlooking Emerald City. It would be an observation camp where he could scout and hone the plan to determine the best way to implement his strategy.

He unsaddled the pack horse draped with Curly's body and dug a shallow grave. He dumped Curly's body wrapped in the tarp into the hole and piled several stones atop the grave, which would keep the body's smell from attracting unwanted coyotes and pumas.

He settled in to wait for the circus that should arrive in two days. And on the second day of his wait, a little before noon, the wagons appeared in the distance.

He left the hill with the pack horse in tow and rode down to join the parade of wagons.

Jack was riding point and saw him from afar. He began waving and pushed his horse into a gallop, soon pulling abreast of Jericho. "Good to see you, boss," Jack commented. "I want you to know the people sure loved me in Clarendon. Those people know real talent when they see it. They adored me. They appreciate me a hell of a lot more than you do."

"That's all I need, a partner with a big head. Now you have a bigger head than you had already. Someone who thinks everyone loves him," Jericho replied, smiling.

They both got down from their horses and began walking them toward the wagons. Jericho told Jack the plans he and Running Wolf had agreed upon and explained, "The one thing we've got to do is make sure these show people are safe and out of the way while we are around them. There's bound to be a lot of gunfire when this plan gets started, and they could be hurt just being close to us."

Jack shook his head, removed his hat, and wiped the sweat from his eyes, saying, "Let me get this all straight in my mind. We first have to rile up Chester Adkins and find a way to rid him of his wealth. Then we must rile up his troops enough to lure them out of town and try to capture as many as possible. You want to put them in chains to transport them back to Fort Justice. And all this without getting us killed in the process?"

Jack got a painful expression and began rolling his eyes to the sky. He looked at Jericho, and his infectious smile returned as he replied, "Seems like a reasonable plan to me. I especially like the part where we piss his men off and kick their ever lovin asses."

Jericho had to marvel at his partner. Most men would have thought his plan crazy and wouldn't have wanted to risk their lives against such great odds.

They slowly walked their horses into the Circus camp. As they entered, everyone waved. The two men secured their horses, and Amanda appeared. She began hugging Jericho, and when she kissed him, she exclaimed, "Hurry up, both of you. You're just in time. Lunch is ready."

"Honey, I hope you're here to stay. I can't survive another day without you. I don't want you ever to leave me alone again."

Jericho's brow furrowed, and he wondered what he had gotten into with this lady. She had a death grip on his arm. It was so tight that it would soon cut off the circulation if she didn't let up soon. He began to think of a way to gently let her down, knowing he would eventually leave to return to Fort Justice.

After the noon meal, Jericho left Jack with the horses and talked with John Prentice. And, of course, Amanda was still draped over his arm.

Jericho explained his plan to both of them. He wondered if the Circus would suffer financially when they removed Mr. Adkins and his cutthroats.

John Prentice assured Jericho that they would be fine. They were better off before Adkins took over the town. The Show's money stream was always derived from the good citizens of a city, not from the likes of Chester Adkins. He explained that most of his traveling troupe were retired circus folks from the East. They had plenty of their own money. They just toured with him for something to do and the adventure of being out in the Wild West.

Jericho warned that his plan would be dangerous for everyone. He explained that he and Jack would execute their plan on the third day of the Circus's engagement in Emerald City. Jericho asked John Prentice to ensure the show's people were safely out of the way when all hell broke loose.

For Jericho's plan to work, several things needed to happen — and they needed to happen quickly. First, they needed to isolate Chester Adkins from his troupe. Second, they needed to locate the money he was using to finance all his illegal operations. Finally, they needed to destroy Adkins's entire empire.

Jericho was sure he knew where that money would be. He remembered what the banker in Dallas had told him about a new safe being delivered to Adkins. Once Jericho found out that Adkins owned the bank, he was sure that would be where the money was stashed. However, the problem remained with how they would lure the gang of deputies or anyone else who supported Adkins into the open.

His plans for luring the gang out in the open centered on Adkins's greed. If Jericho could think of a way to dangle a big payday or maybe remove a big chunk of the man's riches, he was sure that Adkins would fall all over himself to satisfy his greed. He finally put those thoughts away in his mind for now. He would let the ideas float around there until something solid emerged.

CHAPTER TWENTY-SIX

Jericho found Jack just outside the cook's tent, leisurely currying his horse. They used this time together to finalize the execution of Jericho's plan. The best part of the plan that Jack liked was the part about destroying Adkin's wealth.

Jack knew that greed had a way of making people mean and even betraying their beliefs. Sometimes, they betray others and even break the law to satisfy their insatiable need for money. Jericho's plan against Adkins's greed would indeed work against him. The lack of wealth would surely be a way to set a trap for him and his men.

They both walked over to where John Prentice was checking over the wagons. While the men talked, the circus boss explained that they were preparing for tonight's show at Emerald City.

Jericho was curious about Chester Adkins's relationship with the townspeople and asked, "I've been surprised by the fact that the people of Emerald City don't have issues with Adkins and his men."

John answered, "Adkins is very smart in that way. He doesn't let his gang of deputies push the townspeople around too much. And he doesn't demand too much from businesses."

John Prentice added, "But I know the townspeople fear him just the same. There have been whispers and rumors of killings and people disappearing mysteriously. There's nothing solid that would point to Adkins. There sure aren't any witnesses that are willing to come forth.

He also pointed out, "Adkins owns about everything in that town. The bank, the saloon, and the general store. Those are the enterprises I know of. I'm sure there may be more he's involved with that have his backing in some fashion."

John Prentice gave Jericho the information that was the key to his plan when he said, "Adkins has a huge cattle ranch about ten miles out of town. I've never seen the ranch but heard from the town folk. It's quite an operation."

That bit of news was what Jericho had been looking for. He looked at Jack, and it seemed that Jack had reached the same conclusion. Jericho and Jack then asked to be excused, and the two men rode out until they were out of sight of the circus operations.

Jericho turned north, leading Jack to where he had hidden Curly's body. They took up a position, looking down over the town. They had a good view of the Circus grounds, too. They sat on some large boulders and began working on a plan that now included Adkins' Ranch.

This would be a big blow to the man's assets, which Jericho would target. The ranch would be the start and key to destroying his ill-gotten empire.

They both concluded that a trip to Adkins' ranch was the most prudent thing they could do that evening. Their journey would give them insight into what they needed to develop or change in their plans. They expected to arrive just as the sun was setting. The darkness would hide them as they took their first look at Adkins' wealth. Jericho figured there should be enough light to allow them to see the layout of the ranch, livestock, and other parts of the spread.

The two men spent the rest of the afternoon observing the Circus Wagons enter a large area outside Emerald City. They watched as the big circus tent was being erected. It was quite an operation to see. The roustabouts of the circus, along with their teams of horses, didn't waste any effort as they went about their assigned tasks. Within a couple of hours, the tent was fully erected, and the roustabouts were toting parts of the bleachers into the tent. All would be ready for the troupe of circus performers when they arrived.

As dusk began to turn into the first stage of darkness, Jericho and Jack arrived at the Adkins Ranch. They positioned themselves just outside the cattle pens that made up a large portion of the north part of the ranch. They moved stealthily to different locations along several pens. They could see the six sentries positioned about two hundred yards apart. From what they both could observe, the sentries seemed bored. Some were smoking. No one was paying attention to their appointed tasks. They were probably thinking, who in their right mind would dare steal from Adkins?

Jericho and Jack stepped through the rails of the furthest pens. It was now under the cover of darkness. The two men began creeping among the milling cattle.

"Over here," whispered Jack as he patted the side of one of the steers. Jericho looked at the spot on the back portion of the cow where Jack was pointing. "Isn't that your family's brand?" he whispered.

"You're right; that five-point star with three J's in the center is ours. I'll bet that half these cows are ours."

Jericho began moving through the mass of cows, bumping them out of the way as he plowed further into the pen. He was looking for what he was sure he would find. Motioning for Jack to come over to where he had cornered another steer, he whispered, "This one is a Comanche steer."

"See the knife marks by the back of the left haunch that looks like an X with two crisscrossed pointed arrows? That's their marking, all right. Most people wouldn't know where to look. I learned early on, as a member of the Comanche Tribe, where and how to mark their steers. This was another of my father's ideas."

"My father convinced Running Wolf that marking the Tribe's cattle would be the best way to protect what was theirs."

Jericho grabbed Jack and began pulling him to the north end of the pens, explaining in hushed tones, "This is how we're going to rile up Adkins and his men." Then he explained what he had concluded from seeing the number of cows: They would re-steal all the cattle. Later, they would get them all back to their rightful owners. Stealing these cattle back would be a significant financial loss to Adkins if he lost these steers.

Jericho thought Adkins would move heaven and earth to mobilize his people, including the gang of town deputies. He would want those cows back as quickly as possible, and this would be their chance to trap Adkins and his men. The two men retreated from the pens and returned to their horses. They had critical information about the ranch's size and layout.

Jericho started to wonder, however, where all the ranch hands were. They would have to know where those men were when the raid began. He saw movement through the lighted window in the ranch house. He quickly changed their plans and led Jack to the back of the ranch house.

When the two men entered the kitchen via the back door, they were both surprised by a family of Mexicans. The Mexican man was short and chubby, and the Mexican woman with him was as plump as the man. Jericho held up his finger to his mouth. He told them in whispered tones not to yell.

The man and woman cringed in fear, but Jericho was able to calm them and began asking questions that needed answers.

"Who else is in the house?" Jericho asked.

"No one else," replied the chubby man. "We are just the servants. Mr. Adkins brought us here last year. We were taken from our home and sold into slavery by a bad man named Pecos, something or other. Pecos sold us to Mr. Adkins. Mr. Adkins is a very mean man. He beats my Maria if she doesn't clean and cook well enough for him. I help with the cooking and cleanup after all the ranch hands and guards have gone," replied the man.

"Where are the rest of Adkins' ranch hands?" Jericho asked.

"They all go to town every night after the supper meal. All except the guards, that is. Mr. Adkins has guards at all times while the others are away," stated the Mexican man.

Jericho made a quick decision, saying to the man and his wife, "Get your belongings and do it quickly."

Jericho asked the woman, "Do you know where Adkins might have stashed some money around here?"

The man and his wife took them into Adkins' study. They both pointed to a large desk sitting by one of the windows. Jericho rummaged through the desk and found almost nine hundred dollars tucked away in the back of one of the desk drawers.

Putting the wad of bills in Maria's hands, he told her, "Take this money; it's yours, and let's just say, this is for all that grief Adkins and his men put you through." Jericho then told the two servants, "Follow us out of here. Adkins Ranch is about to be up in smoke. Anyone left will be in a world of hurt. It would be best if you left now," Jericho stated.

The couple didn't wait for any more instructions. They threw clothes and personal items into a sack and fled from the ranch house to where Jack held two horses he had taken from the barn. These were horses he had brought for the two Mexicans to ride. He had released all of the other horses. Jack had set several bales of hay on fire.

Jericho hurriedly helped the two servants get on the horses. He instructed them, saying, "You should head south, away from the front of the house. No one will be able to see you from that angle. They should all be busy looking at the backside of the steers and dealing with the fire in the barn. They won't be paying attention to the house."

CHAPTER TWENTY-SEVEN

Jericho waited while Jack and the two servants rode to a place clear of the Adkins Ranch. He watched as the flames engulfed the barn. He quickly rode to where Jack and his two Mexican charges were waiting.

He told the couple, "Keep going south until you reach a place or town you know. Then, and only then, will you be safe."

Jericho and Jack watched as the two servants began their journey into the night. The two men returned to the hilltop where Curly was buried. Later that night, they ate beef jerky, usually reserved for a cold supper. There would be no fire for warmth tonight.

As they lay in their bedrolls, Jericho looked at Jack and explained what might happen in the next part of the plan. "Let's rest now. We might not get much sleep in the days to come. Now that I've seen Adkins Ranch and those sentries, I will change some things in our plan."

"The cattle Adkins has penned up must be near two thousand head or more. Tomorrow, I will return to see Running Wolf. I'm going to ask for help from the Comanche. We shouldn't have too much trouble with Adkins' guards when the Comanche join us. The problem will be that we will probably have to kill some of them. I don't want the guards around when all those steers somehow get loose."

Jericho explained that he needed Jack to show up for his act at the show the next day. "I will be back sometime tomorrow night or the next. When I talked with Running Wolf, I realized I must make changes."

Jericho left well before dawn for the trip to the Comanche camp. He knew the changes to his plan would produce a much more effective outcome. The Comanche Braves would play a significant role as they stole the cattle from the pens at the Adkins Ranch.

They would have to separate everyone's cattle later. But for now, he would have them drive all the cattle into a spot where they could be controlled. Jericho had just the place in mind.

Once he arrived at the Comanche camp, Running Wolf greeted him with sad news. They had been raided by Adkins' men the day after he had left. Adkins' men had killed four more of the Comanche, and Running Wolf thought they might have raided the Starr Ranch. Hearing this latest bad news, Jericho and Running Wolf left immediately for the Starr Ranch.

Jericho explained what he had learned at Adkins' ranch as they traveled. They neared the Starr homestead. Jericho could see black smoke rising ahead of them.

"That smoke's got to be near the ranch house," exclaimed Jericho.

Both men urged their horses into a full gallop as they approached the ranch. They came upon a group of Indian riders who were leading several horses with dead bodies draped over their saddles. The lead rider broke away from the group and came abreast of Jericho and Running Wolf, exclaiming, "Senor Starr. There was a raid on the ranch last night. I sent some other Indian riders to help defend the women and children at the main house. While fighting the raiders, I could see that black smoke for a long time. It makes me worry that there has been a lot of trouble at the house. Please, Senor Starr, you must hurry."

The two men didn't wait another minute. They quickly urged their horses into a hard run. James ran onto the porch as they neared the ranch, shouting, "Jericho, I'm so glad to see you. Please hurry. White Fawn has been wounded. It all happened during the skirmish with Adkin's gang."

"I've got our sisters tending to her wounds. And I saw who was leading the raid. It was Chester Adkins himself. I think he's the one who shot White Fawn when she was trying to free the horses from the barn."

Through his tears, James stated, "I'm personally going to kill that son of a bitch as soon as I can arrange things here and bury our dead."

Jericho and Running Wolf got off their horses and quickly followed James into the house. Jericho saw the carnage scattered all around the room. Inside the house, the air was heavy and thick, with the smell of gunpowder and burning lumber.

He entered the bedroom where they had his mother, rushed to White Fawn, and kneeled by her bedside. Jericho took White Fawn's hand, smiled into her eyes, and asked, "Are you all right, little mother?"

"I will be fine now that you are here, my son," she replied, holding back tears. "I have excellent caregivers," she said, pointing to the two women beside the bed.

Rising, Jericho put his arms around his sisters and thanked them for all they had done for their mother.

With a tremor in his voice, Jericho turned to his brother James and stated, "Brother, I beg you. Please don't leave the ranch now. I know you want to retaliate for what Adkins has done, but right now, you've got to stay here with the family."

"Running Wolf is outside, and he is with me today because Adkin's gang raided the Comanche also. Some of his people were killed, too."

The Comanche people also want justice for these crimes. "Brother, you have my word. Chester Adkins and his gang will never kill anyone again!"

Later that day, the fires were put out, and the horses were back in the corral. Everyone seemed safe.

Jericho and Running Wolf left the ranch and returned to the Comanche Nation. Once they were in camp, Jericho explained the new plan to Running Wolf and his men. "I'll need ten of your braves to help me rustle the cattle held in the pens at Adkins' ranch. I believe most of those steers there probably belong to my family. Some belong to the Comanche. It doesn't matter. We are going to get back what's rightfully ours."

Jericho explained when and where the Braves were to meet him. "In two days, the braves must leave to join me. They need to leave after sunrise. That will give them enough time, and they should arrive just before dark at the north end of the Great Prairie Basin. It's the part of the Basin where the giant boulders overhang the water's shore. Have them bring unlit torches."

After sharing a meal with his grandfather, Jericho returned to where Jack and the circus were set up outside Emerald City. He had been gone two days. His arrival was just in time for the show's last act to begin. He heard the ovation from the crowd, which signaled that Jack had entered the circus tent and was about to perform. Jericho didn't want to miss his partner's performance. This might be the last time he would see how good Jack was with all his weapons.

Amanda saw him by the side of the tent and came running over, crying and smiling all at once. "Jericho, Jericho, I've missed you so much. I was worried that something would happen to you, and I would never see you again."

It was time to tell her that things were going to change. She might be right; she might never see him again, especially if his plans for Adkins backfire. Jericho tried to soothe her, saying,

"Honey, I'm glad to see you too. But the circus is going to have to do without Jack tomorrow. I need him with me."

The noises in the tent quieted and became a low murmur. Jack began to ride around, waving his rifle and shouting a showman's greeting to the crowd. "Hi, everyone, and welcome to the show."

Jack gigged his horse into a trot and brought his rifle to his shoulder. He aimed and fired at the first target, a small white wooden ball dangling from a small rope. The ball fell to the ground and bounced once. Jack had cut the small rope holding the ball from horseback. Jericho was impressed. He told Amanda, "That was quite a shot."

The crowd roared and acknowledged Jack's feat with loud applause. Jack rode and shot his pistol and rifle at various targets without missing. He only stopped long enough to reload and allowed the helpers to place more targets for him. The final part of the act would end the show. Jack's last targets were silver dollars tossed into the air. Two different helpers were set ten feet apart. Jack dismounted and readied himself, drawing his Navy Colt. The workers threw the coins into the air, and Jack fired at both coins. Each of his shots produced a hole in the middle of the coins. The coins fell to the floor of the tent.

Jack continued shooting the dollar coins until his gun was empty — six shots and six coins. He and his helpers gathered the coins, and he walked over to the stands. They began distributing the coins to the children in the stands. It would be a great memento of their day at the circus. Jack remounted and rode out of the tent. The crowd cheered and whistled as he exited.

CHAPTER TWENTY-EIGHT

Jack rode to where Jericho and Amanda were talking and quickly dismounted. Jericho clasped Jack's hand and, slapping him on the back, proclaimed, "Partner, that's the best demonstration of shooting I've ever seen." Jack almost blushed.

Jack was more concerned with something that he had on his mind, and he kept trying to get Jericho's attention with his eyes.

Finally, Jericho realized Jack wanted to talk with him alone and told Amanda that he and Jack must make plans for the next day and excuse themselves.

"Man, have I got some bad news," Jack stated when they were alone. "The gang of deputies has a new leader. I guess Adkins assumed something had happened to Curly. He probably thought he was captured or dead, so he brought another guy. We already heard about this guy. You know the name—Pecos Pete."

"Remember, that's the guy the Mexican man and wife at the ranch talked about. He's the one who sold them to Adkins in the first place. I found out that Pecos Pete is not his real name. It's Peter Johnson. That name is on many posters. He's wanted all over Texas for a bunch of crimes.

"He's a notorious hired killer. The last time I heard about him, he'd been hired by the Stockman's Association in Culver City to drive homesteaders off their lands. I've seen other posters where he's wanted for killing several women. I remember him from when I was a Ranger. He doesn't have a lick of compassion when he kills. He's also wanted dead or alive for killing a Ranger two years ago. This guy is one mean son of a bitch, and now there's no telling what Adkins has planned."

"Where did you learn all this?" asked Jericho.

Jack answered and told Jericho he had visited the saloon owned by Adkins, saying, "I was having some drinks with some of the other circus performers. This guy named Pecos Pete came into the bar and began bragging to some of the deputies about all the people he'd killed.

"Last night, I heard one of the deputies tell another deputy that Adkins had found out his brother was in jail in Dallas," Jack said; he couldn't quite make out all the conversation, but he had heard enough. Adkins was planning a raid on the Dallas jail to break his brother and his men out. We must warn Sheriff Pitts before they can harm anyone or carry out their plans," Jack exclaimed.

Jericho furrowed his brow, saying, "That news will probably make me change some of our plans again. Let me think for a minute."

Jericho mulled over possibilities and a way to inform Pitts of a raid on his jail. He knew they couldn't use the telegraph—Adkins would find out. The only thing that came to mind was that he needed someone he could trust to get a message to the sheriff, and he immediately thought of his brother.

"Jack, I've decided to use James to get this information to Pitts. You and I will be too busy out at Adkins Ranch. The other thing is that Adkins controls everything in town. James must ride to another city with a telegraph station and wire Pitts to warn him."

After a brief discussion, they decided to follow the new plans. However, arrangements had to be made before meeting with the Comanche Braves.

He told Jack. "I must return to my homestead tonight, and I'll speak with James. I'm sure he will want to help. He will know what city has a telegraph."

"Was there a mention of when the gang would be leaving for Dallas?" asked Jericho.

Jack replied, "I thought they would be leaving tomorrow morning, right after breakfast, but I don't know the exact time; they didn't mention that little detail."

Jericho realized he had to work fast and told Jack, "I'm leaving now. I need to get there in time to have James ride out tonight. The wire should be there ahead of the gang. I'll try to return before tomorrow evening's last show. If I'm not, you can figure it out. I probably got too busy. And don't worry about me. This whole mess may get worse before it gets better. We have a lot of irons in the fire and things in play that need to get done quickly. Hopefully, without further distractions, I hope." Jericho replied, looking grim.

His ride to the Family Ranch became a race. He pushed the big animal hard until the homestead lights came into view.

James had been sitting on the porch with a shotgun across his knee. He stepped down to greet Jericho as he slid off his horse. "Thought you would be gone for a while," James said.

"I'm sorry, brother," replied Jericho, "but I don't have much time to explain. I need you to do something right now without asking too many questions."

After explaining the urgency of the matter in Dallas, James told Jericho that Crystal City had a telegraph station. Jericho and James left quickly for the stable to get a fast horse for the trip. A few minutes later, James was on his way into the darkness.

The moon was in their favor. That night, it was full, and its brightness helped James travel, making the ride less treacherous. Soon, he was out of sight.

Jericho returned to the ranch house to check on his mother's injury. White Fawn was sitting up in bed. She had heard his voice when he was talking with James. She was waiting for him to come into her room. As he entered, she motioned for him to sit beside her.

"I'm fine, I'm fine," she reported. "Jericho, would you check on the safety of the ranch hands? They're so brave. I don't know what would have happened if our Indian workers hadn't been here to protect us from that devil Atkins and his men."

Jericho kissed his mother on the cheek. He left the house and began riding around the ranch, checking its defenses. He met with Miguel Alfonzo, the ranch's foreman. Jericho told him about his plans to bring back the stolen cattle but also explained that the Indian workers should be ready for another raid if Jericho's plan failed. Satisfied that everything was prepared at the ranch, he rode to the hill overlooking Emerald City and dug up Curly.

"Curly is a little gamey," he mused, "but just right for what Curly's body would add to the plan."

Everything seemed back on track as Jericho lashed Curly securely to the pack horse. He hoped the horse wouldn't cause him too much of a problem carrying a body, but he couldn't help feeling sorry for the poor horse with Curly's nasty smell. With the body in tow, he rode into town sometime after midnight. He kept to the shadows along the backs of the buildings until he was behind Atkins's bank.

Unlashing the body from the pack horse, he wrestled the load to the ground and opened the tarp with Curly's body. He had to step back from the rank odor for a moment.

He grabbed the tarp's corners and dragged it to the back door. Jericho managed to jimmy the door open and stepped into the gloom until his eyes adjusted to the near blackness. But thanks to the full moon, enough light came through the windows, and he could navigate the building. He went through the bank's interior until he found the door to Adkins's office, opened it, and went back to retrieve Curly's body. Jericho pulled the tarp and the body through the back door and began dragging it into Adkins's office.

Jericho went to great lengths to keep the body away from his clothes, using the tarp to cover Curley's body completely. He didn't want that stink on his clothes, if possible. He wrestled the body in the tarp into the big, overstuffed chair beside the desk.

His stomach was churning as he went outside for fresh air. He retrieved a rope from his saddlebag and fashioned it into a noose. He then returned to the bank to finish the unpleasant task he had set out to do. He placed the looped noose over Curly's neck. He wrapped the remainder of the rope around the body, ensuring it wouldn't fall. It would take some doing to get Curly out of that chair. He searched the desk and found writing materials. He made a sign saying:

This is what happens to thieving cattle rustlers!

Finding a letter opener on the desk, he stabbed the opener and the note into Curly's chest. Jericho left the office and quietly closed the back door. He was sure glad that morbid job was done. He mounted his horse, gathered the pack horse's reins, and left the bank.

It was time to find a spot to rest until tomorrow. The next day should prove to be a big day, full of surprises — plenty of surprises that would cause Adkins a lot of confusion and problems. Jericho opted to return to the hilltop overlooking Emerald City. He slept until an hour past sunrise. He had chosen the hard ground instead of being with Amanda. He knew that if he were with her, there would be endless questions that he wanted to avoid discussing right now. Jericho fixed a cold breakfast for himself. Soon, the sun was fully up, and the temperature began rising. Jericho felt the air getting warm quickly.

The day promised a cloudless sky, but it would be a scorcher. An hour later, Jericho eased his horse off the knoll. He entered the circus grounds, hoping against hope that he wouldn't bump into Amanda. But fate was fickle in these matters, and of course, she found him before he reached the circus tent.

"Where have you been?" demanded Amanda. "I waited all night for you. What was so damn important that you couldn't come to see me like you promised?"

"Amanda," Jericho pleaded, "I can't tell you what I was doing or why I didn't come to your wagon last night. You have to trust me when I say it's for your own good and the good of the circus that I had to stay away. Please don't make a fuss, honey. Things will be fine in a few days. Wait and see."

CHAPTER TWENTY-NINE

Those were not the words Amanda anticipated, and she stormed off, not waiting for any other response from him. Jericho could see she was furious. This was not the time or place for him to make amends.

Jericho tracked down Jack and told him all that had happened since their conversation. "You did what? With Curly's body? And his body is in Adkins's office?" Jack asked, his voice incredulous. "Jericho, you have a very sick mind," Jack laughed out loud, choked, and began coughing until he could clear his throat of phlegm. Recovering, Jack sputtered between laughs. "Damn, I would give my left eye to see the expression on that asshole Adkin's face when he came into that office. Where in the hell do you get all these strange ideas from? Jericho, you have a funny, crazy streak. I am not sure you're in your right mind sometimes."

"Jack, I'll meet you in the saloon tonight after your last show. Maybe we'll find out the impact my little stunt produced." Jericho grinned back in response.

"Boss, before you go, I have more bad news. A whole lot of things have happened since yesterday," Jack said with worry in his eyes.

"That Pecos Pete character... He started the night off with a bang. He beat the hell out of two of the helpers from the circus last night. It seems one of the workers bumped into this Pete feller. He inadvertently spilled his beer, and that started the beatings. If it hadn't been for some townsfolk stepping up, they might be dead now."

"I also heard all the circus workers and roustabouts want revenge, and there's talk that they might try to get back at whoever did this to their friends last night."

"Seems all you do is continually give me bad news," lamented Jericho. "I'm just kidding, Jack," he smiled at the big man. But he saw Jack's face belied his demeanor. He had upset his partner.

Jericho had to explain quickly. "Jack, you're only doing just what I asked. However, this information will change how and when we continue our plan going forward."

"First, we can't allow the circus workers into the bar where they will surely start a fight. With their attitude, a few of them will be dead by tomorrow."

Those men won't stand a chance against Adkin's hired killers. I think it's time you and I acted. Jericho said, "Jack, I will start something at the Bar. Watch closely for my lead in the saloon tonight. Something like when you backed me against that feller, Kinkade, in MacArthur's Saloon."

Later that afternoon, Jericho went to the saloon that Jack had described. He soon found out he was in the right place. Everyone in the place was talking about the beatings.

Jericho wanted to keep a low profile and found a table in the bar's shadows. From his vantage point, he watched several of the gang of deputies come and go through the batwings. They all wore tin stars on their vests, and two deputies were always together.

He overheard two deputies talking and smiled when he heard them murmur about Curly. It seemed his body had caused quite a stir at the bank. They seemed worried about Adkins.

Two other deputies took their place and added to the news. They said Adkins was furious with everything. He was acting crazy about anyone breaking into the bank and depositing Curly. Since no one had heard or seen anything, he had all the deputies on full alert. Adkins had added stricter orders after the ruckus at his ranch. He wanted everyone to be questioned, especially strangers.

Twice, while he was nursing his whiskey glass, two different sets of deputies wanted to know who he was and where he came from. His cover story as a circus worker kept them at bay. After a while, they got used to seeing him and began ignoring him.

He was also buoyed by the talk of the deputies when they said that the six deputies had been dispatched to rescue Homer Adkins. They had waited before leaving; they had to have breakfast first. There didn't appear to be any rush on their part.

Jericho was sure James should have had plenty of time to send the wire. The message would be there well before the gang could get to Dallas. From where Jericho sat, he could see the shadows lengthen against the light coming into the saloon. He estimated that the time was near the evening hour. He ordered a meal from the bar and relaxed.

Jericho had just finished the meal when Jack ambled through the batwings. He used his rifle to keep the doors open enough for his body to go through.

Jack glanced over at Jericho, shook his head, and shrugged. It was a gesture that Jericho knew meant trouble. Jack hadn't been able to sway the circus workers from a fight. They might be there soon to seek revenge for the savage beatings from the night before.

An hour later, a big, gruff, mean-looking man and two deputies, also wearing tin stars, walked through the batwings. The noise in the saloon ceased.

This had to be the infamous Pecos Pete, Jericho thought.

There was an eerie dead silence as if everyone was holding their breath at the same time. As if on cue, the piano player began to play a melody, and the noises in the room returned.

Pecos Pete was a little bigger than Jack but heavier. Jericho estimated him to be six feet tall or maybe a little bigger. He probably weighed about three hundred pounds — three hundred pounds of hard-packed muscle.

Jericho grimaced to himself. He wondered if his plan might need some more tweaking.

Jericho reset his resolve. He needed this Pecos Pete fellow out of the way tonight. He knew that taking the leadership away from the gang was paramount. He wanted to sow more doubts among the deputies' ranks. These goals were necessary for his plan to move forward.

He nodded to Jack, crooked his head to the left, and, with another nod, motioned Jack to a higher perch up the stairs.

Jericho got up from his table and walked toward the bar. He timed his movements to eventually appear behind Pecos Pete, facing the bar's mirror.

Jericho knew that the man could see him in the mirror's reflection. But that didn't worry him. He walked past and softly said into Pecos Pete's ear, "So, you're the asshole who thinks he's so tough. You are nothing but a piece of shit."

Jericho saw the instant anger flash into Pecos Pete's eyes. The big man swung around to face Jericho. Leering at him, Pete tried to grab a handful of Jericho's shirt. And that was the beginning of all the wrong moves Pecos Pete would make tonight.

Blocking Pete's hand to the side with his left arm, Jericho swung a hard right fist. The blow traveled a short distance, but with power and leverage, the jab went straight into Pecos Pete's nose, and blood began to flow in a steady stream.

Someone shouted, "Fight, fight! Some fool just punched that Pete feller."

"The man's nuts," cried another voice in return. "That Pete guy is going to kill the stranger for sure."

Pete reeled a bit, but he regained his balance just in time. He reset his shoulders, wiped his nose with his sleeve, and drew his right arm back to strike. Jericho rose on his toes, leaned into a power stance, and snapped two quick jabs that hit Pete twice in the face before he could blink. One jab under his left eye and again into his nose. The last punch pushed Pete's nose into a crazy angle, breaking the cartilage. Jericho followed up with a powerful jab to Pete's mouth.

That jab also split both his lips wide open, and it happened before Pete could complete the swing of his arm.

Blood flowed freely from Pete's face, and his eyes welled up with tears; the moisture partially blinded the big man. His balance was off kilter as he wavered again. But he moved forward, pressing to gain an advantage.

Jericho didn't wait for Pete to get near him. He followed up with a powerful right hand that hit Pete's chest near his heart, followed by a vicious left-hand uppercut punch to his chin and then two quick jabs to the man's right eye and nose again. Pete staggered and almost fell.

Jack's grin blossomed into a big smile. His boss was much more than just a fast gun. He was one of the best fighters he had ever seen. Jack thought, *there was no end to Jericho's talents.*

Pete was reeling and tried desperately to cover his face. However, he could not prevent the pounding fists from doing more damage.

Out of the corner of his eye. Jack saw a deputy start to draw his gun. Jack leveled his rifle and fired. As if by magic, the deputy's gun was blasted from his hand and fell harmlessly to the floor.

Jack yelled and declared, "Keep your hands away from them, hog-legs boys. This fight is between that big fellow Pete and the fancy dude. And I better not see anybody put their hands near a gun. I'll have to put a bullet somewhere between your head and belly."

CHAPTER THIRTY

"Hey, fancy man," yelled Jack. "Don't stop now. You can go back to kicking that Pete's fellow's ass if you have a mind to!"

Pete, however, used this brief break in the action to recover some of his senses. He gathered himself and straightened. He began throwing wild punches at Jericho's head, hoping to end the fight with one powerful punch.

Pete's plan didn't work out as he intended. Jericho danced away from the wild punch, and Pete began to realize the man punching him was quick and light on his feet. Jericho dodged and bobbed his head, not giving Pete anything to hit.

Jericho hit Pete with a combination of two lefts and a right. These disastrous, powerful punches sent Pete backward as he staggered to the bar's edge.

Blood was everywhere; a steady stream flowed from Pete's broken nose, his mouth was split open, and both his eyes were cut, bleeding, and swollen. A few more punches and his eyes would completely swell shut.

Just as Pete tried to blink away the blood from his vision, Jericho hit him with another flurry of jabs and then followed up with a wicked right cross that floored Pete.

Jericho stood over the beleaguered deputy boss and yelled, "Get up, asshole, you're a sorry excuse for a tough guy."

Jericho taunted, "You're not as tough as your reputation. I heard you like to hurt people. Why don't you get off your fat ass and see if you can hurt me, you dumb shit?"

Pete struggled to his feet, and Jericho backed off, allowing him to get up. Pete was raging mad, trying to look through swollen, bloody eyes at Jericho.

Everyone in the bar was waiting for Pete to do something besides acting like a punching bag.

The big, beleaguered deputy boss pushed away from the bar's edge and staggered toward Jericho, his fists windmilling, trying to catch his opponent off guard. But Jericho danced out of the way, and as Pete sailed by, he was rewarded with a vicious left-hand punch to his right ear.

Pete moaned from all the punishment he was receiving. This was a beating he wasn't used to getting. His mind couldn't conceive that this stranger was able to hit him so many times. And he could do nothing to stop the blows. His breath was coming in gasps now. He couldn't clear his mind. He stepped back a moment and tried wiping away the flow of blood from his eyes.

Pete lunged forward and swung a vicious but wild punch at Jericho's head.

Jericho was ready. He ducked under the punch and hit Pete with a tremendous right hand to his midsection. The force of the punch doubled the big man over. The next punch hit Pete under his armpit, near his heart again.

Everyone in the saloon heard the loud crack of ribs breaking. Pete gasped and winced in obvious pain.

Most broken ribs don't allow anyone to take deep breaths, and Pete was no exception. He couldn't get enough air. He gasped in utter agony, his face turning a pale ash color. He reached out his hand to grab the bar's edge, but all he managed to catch was useless air.

Pete's eyes rolled back into his head. Standing there, almost unconscious, with his arms at his side, he fell face-first and crashed onto the floor, further crushing his broken nose on the bar rail on the way down.

Jericho was both relieved and pleased that the fight seemed to be over. He bent over to check on the prone Pete.

One of the deputies got his courage back and began to draw his gun in an attempt to arrest Jericho or kill him for that stupid act. The deputy got two bullets fired into each of his boots. A howl of distress came from the hobbled man as he joined Pete on the floor. Jericho smiled, thinking *Jack was looking out for him just fine.*

Jericho looked at the remaining deputy and said, "Mister, before you do something stupid, you'd better help your friend with the holes in his feet. And while you're at it, find somebody else to help you cart off Pete."

"You can tell your boss, Mr. Adkins, he's next," Jericho stated.

Jack descended the stairs and said, "I hope somebody starts tending to Pete's wounds before he dies. That asshole's blood is surely making a big mess on the floor. And you better get yourself and your pals out of here soon. I heard a bunch of angry folks from the circus are looking for Pete's hide."

"I wouldn't want to be anywhere near that guy when the shooting starts."

The murmur of the crowd in the saloon quickly turned to shouts. "Holy shit, did you see what I just saw? That stranger hit Pete so many times that I lost count. I don't remember that Pete feller getting off one good punch."

Another man at the bar said, "I'll bet that when Adkins hears about this fight, he's going to be pissed off and mad as hell."

Jericho knew it was time for him and Jack to leave the saloon. They couldn't wait to stop the circus crowd from doing more harm. They had an appointment with the Comanche Braves to complete the last part of the plan.

Jericho first went through the batwings, with Jack backing out and the rifle ready. They mounted their horses and left the town behind. But they both could hear a riotous group of citizens who had seen it themselves. These deputies were not infallible. The likes of just one man could challenge Adkins's authority.

The two men headed for the place where they would meet the Comanche Braves. Jack was full of questions. He was beside himself and couldn't contain his thoughts any longer. "Let's stop right here." He brought his horse to a stop. "Okay, where did you learn to fight like that? And when were you going to tell me about this hidden talent?" Jack demanded.

Jack took off his hat, and with a sweeping motion, bowing in the saddle, he said, "You, sir, are the master of understatement. I heard you say you were ready to stir things up. If that indicates your abilities, you are the world's best. Mr. Adkins will be beside himself after today's happenings."

Jericho wanted to continue moving, but he knew Jack wouldn't be satisfied until he explained and answered his questions. "I learned how to fight as a boy of the Comanche, but I learned how to box at West Point Military Academy. During my first year there, the upper-level students taunted me. They found out I lived with Indians. They didn't take kindly to that, and I had to prove myself several times before they left me alone.

A Captain Jenkins came to see me. He heard about my fights with the upper-level students and wanted me on his boxing team. After months of training, I became the Academy's Champion and held that title for four years straight. Captain Jenkins was a good man and an excellent coach. He was a champion bare-knuckle fighter in his own right. And I became his star pupil. His coaching and a hundred or so fights later taught me the art of boxing."

His words still have meaning to me. He used to say, "Boxing is hand quickness, the location of your punches, and how much force to apply to whatever combination of blows will do the most damage."

Jack seemed satisfied, and they continued to ride until they encountered the Comanche braves carrying torches.

Jack thought to himself, This will be a first for me. I've been fighting Indians as a Ranger almost all my life. It's going to take some getting used to seeing that many braves with war paint and not having to fight for my life.

Jericho conversed with the braves in the Comanche language for a while. Jack could make out some of the words, but knowing the plans, he got the gist of what Jericho expected from his conversation with the Braves.

Jericho left the braves and rode beside Jack. He told him what he had said to the Braves. They would break into smaller groups of five. Jericho would be in charge of one group, and Jack would be in charge of the other. He assured Jack that when they arrived at the Adkins ranch, the braves he would send with him knew enough of our language to follow his orders.

It was dark as they approached the cattle pens. The cows sensed their presence and began to bawl and fidget even more. Jericho took five braves with him to take out the guards. He left the other five with Jack, who would stay back and provide cover. He told Jack they would reassemble once they removed the guards. Jericho and his braves made short work of the guards without firing a shot. Comanche braves with knives were silent, expert killers.

Jericho and his group rode quickly to where Jack and his group were waiting. Jericho put a flint to his torch. Once it was fully ablaze, he rode to each brave, lighting their torches. As instructed, the braves fanned out in a semicircle around the pens. They began waving the torches and firing their weapons in the air in unison.

The fire, smoke, and gunshots spooked and panicked the cattle into a frenzy. The whole mass of penned-up steers broke through the fences and began to stampede. The next part of the plan was to herd the cattle toward the general direction of the natural box canyon. If the plan worked, the herd would eventually end up in the canyon about twelve miles south of the Adkins Ranch.

CHAPTER THIRTY-ONE

Once the cattle were on a dead run, Jack and his group of braves stopped providing support and began setting fires on all the wooden structures on the ranch. Jack made sure the ranch hands and the animals in the ranch buildings were clear of all structures before the fires were lit. However, that allowed some of the ranch hands to galvanize into action. They began firing at the eerie, ghostly shapes holding the smoking-lit torches.

Jack stopped and waved his group of braves forward to complete their tasks. He set himself in his saddle and began providing cover fire with his rifle. His accuracy quickly made the ranch hands dive for cover. Soon after, their firing ceased.

Jack's job was to wing the ranch hands. He didn't want to kill anyone, but his presence with the rifle kept them at bay. They weren't getting paid enough to risk getting their heads blown off for Adkins.

The empty barns were the first to become a mass of burning timbers. Next were the bunkhouses. Finally, the main house became fully engulfed in flames. Soon, the Adkins ranch, the keystone of his empire, would be gone.

Jericho and his crew of braves managed to turn and direct the herd toward the box canyon, but the cattle remained a frenzied, stampeding mass. Looking over his shoulder, Jericho saw the devastating destruction of the Adkins ranch. Everything that could burn was in flames.

In the meantime, Jack had begun to ease up on his withering rifle fire. Most of the ranch hands were now running away. No one was firing at him or the Indians anymore. He let them escape into the safety of the fields surrounding the ranch.

There would be no attempt to put out this fire. Anyone who could have helped extinguish the fire was gone, Jack thought to himself. It didn't matter anyway. The fire was well beyond anyone's capabilities now. The Adkins empire was a blaze of fire that could be seen for miles.

Jack was about to ride off. His work at the ranch was done. However, he saw that two ranch hands had found some wandering horses, and they were speeding away, riding bareback.

Jack was sure these men were headed for Emerald City. That would be the final thing that needed to happen for Jericho's plan. Someone had to deliver the fire's message. Adkins would need to find out the bad news quickly. Those riders would be the messengers.

Meanwhile, Jericho looked at the dug-up trail the cattle had made. The steers had done precisely what he had hoped. They had produced a gigantic trail that should be easy to follow. Several thousand stampeding cattle left a pretty big mark on the landscape. A blind man could find the way without much difficulty.

Three hours later, the cattle had worn themselves out sufficiently, and both riders and steers were tired. They were exhausted enough that the animal's fast pace had become a slow walk. A while later, the herd entered the mouth of the natural box canyon that Jericho had selected. This box canyon would be the perfect place for the final part of his plan. Once they reached the far end of the canyon, the cattle would be in a natural pen. They were his bait.

Jericho was sure Adkins wouldn't stand for someone doing to him what he had been doing to others. The trap was set. Running Wolf and several of his braves were already in position. They were above him on the ridge, able to see down from their vantage point overlooking the box canyon entrance.

The braves with Jericho were his mounted cavalry. They all rode into a line of trees across from the mouth of the Box Canyon. It was a perfect place to hide both horses and riders. Jack and his group showed up several minutes later. Jericho rode out quickly from the trees and led them to where the other braves were waiting, hidden in the trees.

The ground force was now complete. They were twelve strong—a force that would close the trap once Adkin's men entered the box canyon. The little force didn't have long to wait. The thunder of Adkin's men's horses could be heard well before anyone could see them.

Looking up at the now-dark sky, Jericho was thankful for the heavily overcast skies, which would also help conceal his men. He prayed there would be no heavy rains or thunder; he didn't need anything else to spook those cattle.

While Jericho was still thinking about the weather, twenty-five men emerged from the dust cloud, hell-bent on damnation. The riders were pushing their horses hard as they entered the mouth of the box canyon, following the considerable trail left by the cattle. They never stopped to wonder why anyone would drive all those steers into what appeared to be a box canyon.

The canyon's floor stretched about two miles before butting against its rock-faced walls. That's where the cattle had stopped. Several thousand steers stood in a mass, crowded into a considerable semi-circle — a mass of bawling, ornery, frightened critters.

Too late, Adkins's men began to realize something was wrong.

This was too easy. One of the men in the lead signaled a halt. But they were too far into the Box Canyon by that time. They had ridden up on the ass end of the mass of cattle. The man in charge saw the trap and started yelling orders to turn back. But it was far too late.

Jericho, Jack, and their troupe of braves rode out of the trees and entered the mouth of the canyon. Their job was to cut off any retreat of Adkins's gang of men.

Adkins's men had just turned their horses and were about to race out of the canyon. Jericho fired a single shot into the air.

That signaled Running Wolf and his forces to begin firing down on the gang of men.

Adkins's men began racing through the withering rifle fire from above, only to ride into the mounted cavalry that Jericho and Jack commanded.

Jericho's mounted cavalry fired shot after shot into the advancing riders, who were now in utter chaos. Adkins's men fell like flies. A blistering, vicious crossfire was massacring the trapped men. No matter where they looked, weapons were being fired at them. There was no place to find cover.

The attack lasted less than ten minutes. Those of the gang who were still alive began throwing down their weapons. Those who were still able began to raise their hands in the air. More than half of the gang had been killed or wounded while the battle raged. Jericho had his little army of braves surround the remaining few alive. In the end, the final count of Adkins's men alive or only slightly wounded was twelve.

Soon, Running Wolf and his forces joined the others. They all pitched in and began helping bind the men who were alive or wounded. Some began tying the dead bodies to stray horses.

Jack was given the task of locating Adkins. He was the only one of the men Jericho had with him who had ever seen the man. It soon became evident to Jack that Adkins was not among the gang.

Jericho asked Running Wolf to escort the prisoners into Emerald City. He and Jack would then look for Chester Adkins.

The two men rode hard. Jericho couldn't shake the ominous feeling that had come over him. The situation unfolding was unclear. Since Adkins was not with the gang at Box Canyon, could there be more men out there? Everything seemed questionable.

As Jericho and Jack entered Emerald City, they were greeted by a troupe of soldiers. Jericho figured they had been dispatched from Fort Justice.

He was pleased with this new development. Better yet, he knew Lieutenant Golden, the person in charge. He was one of the new officers assigned to Fort Justice just before Jericho went on his mission to find a Deputy Marshal.

Riding close to the mounted officer, Jericho extended his hand and greeted him, saying, "It's good to see you, Lieutenant. Your presence here in Emerald City is perfect timing and my good fortune. I'll have several prisoners for you to escort back to Fort Justice very soon."

Jericho asked, "Did Judge Bidwell send you?"

Lieutenant Golden grinned and said, "Why, yes, he told me you might need the Army to lend a hand. Seriously, he was afraid something had happened to you. He seemed very worried about the both of you."

A while later, the Comanche Braves entered the town with their caravan of dead and alive prisoners in tow.

Jericho saw the fear and distrust in the eyes of the soldiers from the fort. They were face-to-face with Indians with war paint on their faces and guns at the ready.

CHAPTER THIRTY-TWO

"Hold up!" Jericho barked to the assembled Troupes. "Don't anyone do anything stupid? These Indians are my special deputized posse. They have just performed an invaluable service for the people of this town and everybody within this State."

"I'll vouch for them," Jericho stated.

Lieutenant Golden moved his horse closer to Jericho, scratched his head in disbelief, and whispered, "This is the first time I ever faced Indians with guns and war paint that I didn't have to shoot or chase into some hills! That'll be something I can tell my kids—if I ever have any!"

After giving orders to the Lieutenant and telling him what he wanted done with the prisoners, Jericho and Jack left everyone assembled on the main street while they visited the bank.

As they arrived, a small crowd was milling around in front of the bank. Jericho asked one of the men in a butcher's apron, "Has anybody seen Adkins?"

The man with the apron spoke up, saying, "He's gone. And the safe in the bank is wide open. That son-of-a-bitch has taken all the money that was in his bank. A lot of the bank's money was ours," cried another, and the crowd murmured in agreement.

Someone else called out, "There's a dead man behind the bank. It's that feller Pete, the one you fought with. We heard shots, and when we went into the alley, we saw a wagon from the circus. The wagon was hell-bent on tomorrow, with Adkins driving the rig. That's when we saw the body of that fellow Pete on the ground."

Another man said, "I also saw that painted wagon leaving, and four of the so-called deputies left town with him. Adkins was pushing the team as hard as he could."

"Adkins is on the run for sure," Jack commented to Jericho. "There's something very wrong with him having a wagon from the circus to use in his escape."

Jericho agreed, and together, they rode to where the circus had put up their tents. The two men wheeled their mounts around and headed straight for the big tent.

When they arrived, Norma Jane ran up, crying and sobbing uncontrollably. Through gulps of air and half-sobs, she told Jack, "They've taken Amanda and our payroll wagon. It's got all our money in it. Mr. Prentice was shot trying to stop them."

After a while, Norma Jane stopped crying, but it was several minutes before she could explain what had happened. "Adkins and his men rode in here a while ago. They began threatening and causing trouble. We didn't have weapons and didn't want a riot. We're performers, not gun-hands. He was looking for Jack. When he couldn't find him, Adkins took our payroll wagon. Amanda was still in it."

"One of his deputies shoved her dad out of the way as he tried to stop them, and the deputy shot him." Jericho and Jack dismounted and followed Norma Jane to the back of one of the wagons. Looking in, Jericho saw that John Prentice was resting comfortably. He even waved a small hand when he saw Jericho and said, "You've got to get Amanda back, Jericho. Please don't let that scum Adkins hurt her. She's too precious to me. Don't worry about me. I'm going to be okay. Just get my girl back safe."

After a quick check of the surrounding area, Jericho located the tracks left by the wagon. The two men raced their horses in the direction the wagon's tracks were headed. It was evident to Jericho that Adkins wasn't trying to hide or fool anybody with his escape. He was pushing the team hard. They were moving fast to put as much distance as possible between the people of the circus and the people of Emerald City.

"What do you plan to do once we catch up to Adkins?" Jack asked as they followed the wagon's tracks.

"Now that Amanda is a captive of Adkins, we must be more careful with our guns. Who knows what that ass-wipe Adkins might do if he sees our approach?" Jericho responded.

"Our best bet is to ride hard and get ahead of Adkins and his men. If we can do that, we can wait for them and hopefully surprise them at the right moment. I figure they have to keep to this road. And he's pushing the team hard. He's got to change horses soon, so they will probably stop at Melville Junction. There's a stop-over station for the stage in that town. That's where he'll find the replacement horses he will need. And it's a good bet Adkins will get into the Oklahoma Territories."

They pushed their big, powerful horses into a lather as they rode cross-country to pick up valuable time and get ahead of Adkins and the men he had with him.

To Jericho's great relief, Melville Junction had no wagon or gang. They had beaten Adkins to the town.

The two men quickly found the stagecoach stables. They hid their horses and took up positions in the rear of the barn, leading to the stables. There, they would wait for the gang to appear. Soon, they heard the wagon and the riders as they entered the town.

They both heard Adkins shouting instructions. "You two get fresh horses and be quick about it. We might get company. I don't want to be here longer than we have to."

Jericho and Jack waited in the darkness until two deputies entered the barn and entered the stables. They came back, leading a fresh team of horses, and Jack and Jericho crept from their hiding place. They silently approached the two outlaws from behind. Guns poked the ribs of the two deputies, and they heard the threat: "Boys, don't breathe or make any fast moves. I really wouldn't want to kill you. It might scare the horses," Jack said in a low, threatening voice. With guns shoved into both of

Adkins's men's ribs, they paled, did as they were directed, and were relieved of their weapons.

Jack and Jericho quickly went about gagging and tying the Adkins men tightly to the beams holding up the barn.

"Adkins has only two other men by my count," whispered Jack.

"How do you want to play it from here?"

"Jack, I want you to wait here. I'm going to lead these horses out and hide between them," Jericho replied. "Once I'm clear of the doors, you get up in the barn's loft. You try to cover the other two. I want to take care of Adkins, myself, personally."

Jericho put on a hat of one of the men they had tied up. He pushed the stable doors open and urged the horses to move into the street. He hoped to hide between them several yards down the street.

However, Adkins must have smelled something funny about the man leading the team of horses and yelled, "That's not our man!" As he cried out, he drew his gun and fired. On horseback, Adkins's two other men swiveled in their saddles and turned toward where Adkins had fired the shot. Both men had their guns out. They were about to fire on Jericho when a shot rang out, and one of the men on horseback fell off his horse onto the street.

"Don't even try it," Jack yelled at the remaining rider. "At this range, I can't miss." However, after his announcement, Jack had to duck back into the recesses of the loft when Adkins fired up into the open door at him.

Adkins swiveled around to face Jericho, standing between the horses, and fired again. His shot nicked one of the horses in the rump. The four horses all reared in unison. But that was the last thing Adkins ever did on this earth.

Jericho's hand flashed to his Colt and fired, shooting Chester Adkins. The shot hit Adkins right between the eyes. The man slumped forward and fell off the wagon onto the ground. He was dead to the world as he lay face down in the dirt.

Jack reappeared at the door of the loft and pointed his gun at the last man on horseback. Jericho ran to the back of the wagon, and when he arrived, he saw that Amanda was all trussed up with a gag in her mouth. She was lying on sacks of what appeared to be lumpy bags of money.

Jericho hoisted himself into the wagon and took the gag out. He began untying the struggling woman.

"What took you so long?" Amanda growled as she was let loose. "Those men might have killed me at any time along the way. I kept hoping and praying that somebody would save me, but wouldn't you know, it had to be you." Gasping for breath, Amanda began crying, and she asked through her sobs, "Is my dad all right? How bad was he hurt?" All her pent-up emotions got the best of her, and she wailed, crying as the tears streaked down her face.

"Take a deep breath," Jericho said as he tried to calm her. He touched her shoulder for reassurance and said, "Your dad's okay, and you're safe now. Everything turned out for the best. Adkins and his gang of thugs are gone for good."

But even as he tried to reassure her, Amanda grabbed Jericho's hand from her shoulder and turned her back to him. He could tell by her actions and coldness toward him that Amanda was now through with him.

CHAPTER THIRTY-THREE

Amanda continued to glare and pout whenever he was anywhere near her. As they prepared to leave, her words and complaints turned into a major bitch session. Gone was the loving and caring lady he had once known.

However, Jericho needed Amanda to drive the wagon. When he asked her to drive, she started ranting and fussing. She began to cry again as she sobbed, "I'm so sore from lying on those sacks I can hardly move. Now you want me to drive this damn wagon in my condition. How could you be so unfeeling? I've gone through hell today, and you don't care about me at all. You only want me to drive this stupid wagon for you."

Jericho shook his head, knowing that his words to her would bring on more complaining. He tried to distance himself by making an excuse about having to return to the stables. He needed to round up the rest of the gang members who were still alive. The three surviving men were brought to the back end of the wagon. Jack made sure they were securely tied to the wagon's frame. He and Jack began draping and securing the body of Adkins and the other dead gang member to their horses.

Jericho found the stable owner in a nearby saloon. After some hard-fought bartering and upfront money, Jericho traded the old team from the wagon for a fresh new one.

The return trip to Emerald City was uneventful, and shortly after dropping off a still-pissed-off and complaining Amanda, Jericho took over and finished driving the wagon to the back of the bank. A few of the town's citizens helped to unload the money bags back into the bank's safe. It was then that Jericho realized he couldn't lock the safe. He requested two men from Lieutenant Golden to guard the bank vault. He and the rest of the town would have to determine where the money had come from and whose money belonged to whom.

The morning of the next day, Jericho gathered several of the town's merchants together and announced that he was a judge appointed by the State of Texas. He and Jack had been sent to Emerald City to re-establish law and order in the area.

His first official act was to appoint a new sheriff. The town's merchants helped with the selection, and together, Jericho and the new sheriff picked out four new deputies. To make it official, Jericho administered the Oath of Office.

His next official act was to appoint a temporary town council until regular elections could be held.

Later that afternoon, James, his brother, rode into town looking for Jericho. Once he found him, James told him what had happened since his wire to Sheriff Pitts. James had asked Pitts to send him a return wire to see if he had received his message. The sheriff responded by saying, "Thanks for the warning." A few minutes later, another message told James that he had three of Adkin's deputies in jail. It seems that the other three deputies met an untimely death due to lead poisoning.

"I was about to leave the Telegraph Office when Pitts sent another wire, but this one was for you, Jericho. The message said, 'Thanks to you, I had plenty of time to prepare for the raid. My deputies didn't have any casualties or injuries.'"

Buoyed by this information, Jericho focused on a big problem: the money situation. Jericho thought of the banker in Dallas. Now that he could use the telegraph without Adkins knowing the message, he sent a wire to Judge Bidwell. Jericho explained that he needed the judge's influence to persuade a man named Jamison, a reputable banker in Dallas, to come to Emerald City to help sort out the money mess as soon as possible.

The return wire message was short and sweet: "Jamison will be there in two days. Stop."

The next problem was determining the proper owners of all the cattle. Leaving Emerald City, Jericho and James rode to the Comanche camp. Once there, they were invited into the teepee of Running Wolf. The three men were there to decide what to do with all the cattle. Jericho asked both men if they would start culling the Comanche steers from the Starr ranch steers. James and the nearby ranchers would sort out the remaining cattle and return them to their rightful owners.

Banker Jamison arrived in Emerald City by stagecoach two days later. Exiting the coach, he asked the Station Master where he could find Judge Starr. The station manager escorted him to Jericho's temporary office at the bank. When the banker saw Jericho, he complained about the wire from Judge Bidwell and the threat from Sheriff Pitts. He was distraught that Sheriff Pitts told him he would be locked up if he didn't comply and would somehow lose the key. Not knowing if the sheriff was serious or not, he was here to do as Jericho wished.

The banker had settled down after his initial outburst. He was curious why Jericho had asked him to work at this bank in Emerald City. What was so important that he had to leave his own business?

Jericho grabbed the banker's arm and ushered him past the two guards. The two men walked into the room with the safe. When they were in front of it, Jericho swung the unlocked door open and said to the banker, "I believe you can see my dilemma." Jericho pointed to the numerous bags, telling the banker they were full of money, but he didn't know who the money belonged to.

Jericho pointed out the obvious: some of the money belonged to the people of Emerald City, some belonged to Wells Fargo, and some belonged to... whoever. He had no earthly idea who it belonged to.

He told the banker that the money must be sorted out and returned to its owners. Jericho did not want to do this, nor did he have the time to devote to the undertaking, saying, "I sent it to you because you have the expertise. I needed someone who knows the ins and outs of banking and money transactions."

Jericho was impressed by the banker when they were in Dallas. When Judge Bidwell summoned the banker, it was because Jericho trusted the banker to handle the matter. Every transaction had to be recorded and accounted for, as the Army and Jericho's boss were sticklers for accountability.

Jericho continued his instructions to the banker. He suggested that the banker consider opening a local branch of his Dallas Bank here in Emerald City. It would be a good way for the State of Texas to repay Jamison for his invaluable service.

Later, Jericho met Jack in the saloon where he had fought Pete. It was the first time in a long while that they had the chance to sift through everything that had transpired. They ate in silence while they enjoyed their meals. After eating, they began discussing the information in their report to Judge Bidwell.

Jack was philosophical the following morning. "It seemed like only yesterday that we were listening to Judge Bidwell talking about some little problem developing in Emerald City. Some little problem? I sure would hate to see a big problem come his way!"

Jack grinned at his partner, saying, "Jericho, if there's one thing I know for sure, it's that there's never going to be a dull moment around you."

"Trouble must camp outside your door in the morning, waiting with joyous anticipation, ready to follow you the minute you begin your day."

EPILOGUE

Ten days later, Jericho and Jack rode through the gates of Fort Justice. They went immediately to Judge Bidwell's office, ready to present their report.

After several questions from the Judge regarding the money distribution and the new City Council for Emerald City, the Judge was happy the problem with the Comanche deaths had been resolved. He seemed very satisfied and pleased with how well the events had played out.

Judge Bidwell began shaking Jericho's hand, telling him what a great job he had done. They had presented themselves well.

He then grabbed Jack's hand and told him that he could see he would be the best Marshal he had ever hired.

The End

NEW STORY

DAVIS MOUNTAIN COMANCHEROS

Judge Bidwell's face became a deep scowl as he seemed to be wrestling with a heavy burden. His gaze focused on the two law enforcement officers sitting before him. His solemn voice proclaimed, "Jericho, I had hoped that you both would be able to get some rest after your encounter with Adkins. But that's not to be. Something horrible happened yesterday, and I need you both to ride to Midland, Texas, as soon as possible.

"When you arrive, you must check with the town's Sheriff. He'll tell you what happened since his communiqué to me. His wife was most troubling and a big problem for all of us. It involves a Comanchero's raid on a ranch that belongs to a dear friend of mine—Captain Anderson. My friend was severely wounded in the raid, and the most troubling fact is that those marauders took his wife and two daughters. You're the best people I know to help retrieve the wife and the girls. You have experience with the Indian Nation's Tribes. There is an Apache Tribe in that area, and they have information about this group of Comancheros from beyond the Davis Mountains. I was informed that these animals have been traded with the tribe before.

Judge Bidwell explained what the Army had relayed to him and what they knew about the Comancheros. Their leader is a disgraced half-breed, part Apache and part Mexican. "His name is Della De Magnenz. He's evil and a savage killer. He's as tough as they come."

"Your job will be difficult and extremely dangerous, but I think the Apache Tribe might be your best lead to find his family and hopefully return them unharmed." Judge Bidwell talked about his friend, Captain William Anderson. He was a good man while he served at Fort Justice. Just last year, he retired from my Command. He purchased a ranch near Midland, just below the Davis Mountains. The reports say the Comancheros took the wife and the couple's ten-year-old twin girls. The leader is also known to the Mexicans as 'Virgen Malingo.' When we translated it into English, it means 'pure evil."

The Judge explained, "In his wire, Sheriff Marks asked the Commander of the Fort for help by sending a Comanche Scout named Two Feathers. The Comanche Scout had been under the command of Captain Anderson when Anderson was C Troop's Platoon Leader. Anderson asked that Two Feathers be allowed to come and help him track and retrieve his daughters. The Commander of the Fort consulted me, and we both agreed to send Two Feathers.

Judge Bidwell ordered Jericho Starr and Jack Harden to follow up, help in any way possible, and go to the Midland Area as soon as they could be ready. Jericho began thinking about what they were about to tackle. He hoped against all hope that, with the help of Two Feathers, he and Jack wouldn't be too late to save the girls. However, their help was only the beginning of their problems. There would be much more to this story than the abduction and the rescue of the mother and the two girls.

About The Author

I fell in love with stories in books as a youth. I marveled at and fantasized about the many different and exciting outlets these books provided. Ultimately, I settled on stories about the Old West. Westerns became my favorite reading venue, and later, I transitioned to my storytelling. The Old West, with its famous sheriffs, outlaws, and larger-than-life heroes, became my primary source of writing material. I saw how authors brought their characters to life and engaged the reader's imagination in their tales. The historical context of these stories was paramount to my research, and the Old West setting shaped my decision to put the stories in my head onto paper.

My writing name, Peter Beck, is a tribute to the legacy of my ancestors. Peter honors my grandfather on my father's side, a man of great integrity and wisdom, for whom I was named. Beck is my mother's maiden name, representing a lineage of strong, resilient men and women.

This connection to my roots is a constant source of inspiration for my writing.